Applied C# in Financial Markets

Wiley Finance Series

Applied C# in Financial Markets

Martin Worner

John Wiley & Sons, Ltd

Other Wiley Editorial Offices

John Wiley & Sons Inc., 111 River Street, Hoboken, NJ 07030, USA

Jossey-Bass, 989 Market Street, San Francisco, CA 94103-1741, USA

Wiley-VCH Verlag GmbH, Boschstr. 12, D-69469 Weinheim, Germany

John Wiley & Sons Australia Ltd, 33 Park Road, Milton, Queensland 4064, Australia

John Wiley & Sons (Asia) Pte Ltd, 2 Clementi Loop #02-01, Jin Xing Distripark, Singapore 129809

John Wiley & Sons Canada Ltd, 22 Worcester Road, Etobicoke, Ontario, Canada M9W 1L1

Wiley also publishes its books in a variety of electronic formats. Some content that appears
in print may not be available in electronic books.

British Library Cataloguing in Publication Data

A catalogue record for this book is available from the British Library

ISBN 0-470-87061-3

Typeset in 11/13pt Times by TechBooks, New Delhi, India
This book is printed on acid-free paper responsibly manufactured from sustainable forestry
in which at least two trees are planted for each one used for paper production.

Contents

List of Examples

List of Figures

List of Tables

Preface

This book is designed to help experienced programmers into the C# language. It covers all the relevant concepts of C# from a finance viewpoint. In the preparation of this book a small standalone futures and options trading application was written to cover all of the sections of C# that are relevant to finance and the code from the application is used throughout the book to illustrate the topics covered.

The key points covered are focused on building a Windows application in a finance environment. With this in mind there are some sections of C# that have been omitted, for example it is unlikely that C# would be used to connect to exchanges thus in-depth coverage of sockets and TCP/IP package handling has not been included.

The operators, data types and controls are covered to begin with as they form the core section of programming. Object Oriented programming is dealt with in depth from a practical approach and the commonly used concepts are covered. The emphasis of the book is in applying C# to finance and thus it does not cover each topic to its full depth as there are aspects of C# rarely used in financial applications.

In addition to the Object Oriented section, ADO.NET and the simpler I/O sections that may apply to a Windows application are covered along with some basic XML as many financial applications share data using XML.

Recognising that there are large legacy systems within each financial house, written in C++, Java and mainframe, the C# projects that are likely to be undertaken will have to fit in with these systems rather than replace them. C# offers a powerful language in building robust Windows applications that leverages off the Object Oriented concepts without being too complex to manage.

Mobile computing, Web forms and ASP are not covered in this book, as most applications will be written for the desktop. Although some finance houses may use ASP and Microsoft-related Web technologies, this is a topic for another book.

The workshops have been designed to cover the topics in the book and let you have a try, and they aim to build on each other and result in a simple options calculator that allows a trader to perform 'what-if' calculations and switch between models.

I would like to thank the team at theCitySecret Ltd for all their support and encouragement; Jonathan Heitler for keeping me on track, Nick Doan for helping on the modelling and mathematics and Jacky Pivert for trying out all the workshop exercises.

The complete code for the sample Futures and Options trading application used to illustrate the book can be downloaded at http://www.wileyeurope.com/go/worner. Please follow the instructions on the website on how to download the code.

1
What is .NET and how does C# fit in?

C# is one of the family of languages that make up .NET, the idea being that VB programmers could pick up VB.NET easily and C++ or Java developers could move into C# without too many problems. This meant, potentially, that existing teams of VB and C++ or Java programmers could develop code in a familiar language and the compilers organise the code to run together.

Note that C# is case sensitive, thus Console.Write is not the same as console.write.

1.1 .NET FRAMEWORK AND THE COMMON LANGUAGE RUNTIME

The Common Language Runtime (CLR) is the end result of the source code when compiled. However, to get to the CLR the C# source is first compiled into Microsoft Intermediate Language (MSIL). The intermediate language is necessary as this allows the family of languages to all work together (C#, VB.NET, etc.), so in theory developers can work in C#, VB.NET and VC++ .NET simultaneously on the same project.

Once the .NET framework is installed for a platform then the compiled code (CLR) can run on the given platform.

A key feature of the CLR is memory management; whereas in C++ the programmer must ensure that the memory is allocated and released, CLR does it for you.

The class libraries are extensive in CLR with the addition of ADO.NET from the .NET framework.

COM is not supported in .NET although there are some tools to integrate ActiveX controls and DLLs.

Table 1.1 The .NET framework at a glance

VB.NET	C#	C++	J#
	Microsoft Intermediate Language		
	Common Language Runtime		

2

The Basics of C#

Before starting on the object oriented concepts and how these are applied in finance it is worth spending some time looking at the basics of C# and familiarising yourself with the operators, data types and control structures.

First, you will look at the operators to assign, calculate and evaluate conditions. Second, data types are examined, from the built-in types to the objects that represent more sophisticated data. Finally, you will look at how to apply data types and operators in control structures.

2.1 ASSIGNMENT, MATHEMATIC, LOGICAL AND CONDITIONAL OPERATORS

In C#, as in other languages, there are operators to assign values to variables, mathematical operators and operators to compare types. This section covers the operators that are commonly used, and will look at both the use and the precedence of the operators. Later in this section you will see how these operators apply to control structures.

2.1.1 Assignment operator

The assignment operator = is an important operator as in most programs values will need assigning to variables. Note the assignment operator should not be confused with the equality operator ==.

The assignment operator assigns the value right of the operator to the variable left.

Example 2.1: Assignment of variables
```
variable = value;

string newvariable = "hello world";
int newnumber = 10;
```

As Example 2.1 shows the string `newvariable` has been assigned with the value 'hello world'.

Table 2.1   Simple mathematical operators

Description	Operator	Example
Add	+	10 + 2
Subtract	–	10 - 2
Multiply	*	10 * 2
Divide	/	10 / 2

2.1.2 Mathematical operators

The basic mathematical operators are used to perform the simple mathematical computations as shown in Table 2.1.

In Example 2.2 the mathematical operators are shown, as they would be used in a program. The operators may either be used on numbers or variables as the examples illustrate.

Example 2.2: Mathematical operators in use
```
int add = 10 + 10;
double amt = _price * _qty;
double d2 = d1 - v;
double percent = _price/100;
```

2.1.3 Calculate and re-assign operators += –= *= /=

The calculate and re-assign operators are used to perform a mathematical operation on a variable and assign the result. Table 2.2 shows the common calculate and re-assign operators.

The calculate and re-assign operators are used instead of performing a simple mathematical operation on a variable and then assigning that variable to itself using the one combined operator. By using the calculate and re-assign operator the variable performs the mathematical operation and then assigns the results to itself. If, for example, a running total

Table 2.2   Calculate and re-assign operators

Description	Operator	Example
Add and re-assign	+=	int res += 2
Subtract and re-assign	–=	int res -= 2
Multiply and re-assign	*=	int res *= 2
Divide and re-assign	/=	int res /= 2

quantity is required in the program (Example 2.3 illustrates the two approaches) clearly the calculate and re-assign operation is easier to read and requires less typing. Note that the two statements in Example 2.3 are interchangeable.

Example 2.3: Addition and assign

```
qty = qty + quantity;
qty += quantity;
```

In addition to the calculate and re-assign operators there are also two special operators to add (++) or subtract (--) one from the given number or variable. The placing of the operators is important as the order of addition or subtraction and assignment is different. Prefix is when i++ returns the value of i and then increments itself by one, whereas the postfix operator ++i adds one to i and then returns the value. Table 2.3 shows an example of the prefix and postfix operators in use.

Table 2.3   Prefix and postfix operators

Prefix increment operator	Postfix increment operator

```int pre = 1;```
```Console.Write(pre++);```
```Console.Write(pre);```
	```int post = 1;```
	```Console.Write(++post);```
	```Console.Write(post);```

```Output 1``` ``` 2```	```Output 2``` ``` 2```

The prefix and postfix operators are often encountered in loops to increment or decrement a variable, as a shorter way of writing $i = i + 1$; you would write i++. Example 2.4 shows the prefix operator being used in a loop.

Example 2.4: Prefix example in a loop structure

```
for (int i=0;i<categories.Length;i++)
{
   loadFromDB(categories[i]);
}
```

2.1.4   Logical operators

Logical operators are used in programs to compare two values and return a Boolean value. Table 2.4 lists the commonly used logical operators and gives examples of their use and results.

Table 2.4   Commonly used logical operators

Operator	Description	Example	Result
==	equal to	100 == 100	True
>=	greater or equal than	>= 100	True
>	greater than	100>100	False
<=	less than or equal to	100<=100	True
<	less than	100<100	False
!=	not equal to	100 != 100	False

A simple example is to use the equality operator to compare the value of a string variable with a string, as shown in Example 2.5, with the result being assigned to a Boolean variable.

Example 2.5: Equality operator
```
bool activeAccount = acctCat == "A";
```

A more realistic example, as seen in Example 2.6, is the evaluation used in the context of an if statement. You will learn more about if and control structures later in the section.

Example 2.6: Equality operator in a control structure
```
if (_rates.Count == 0)
{
   getRatesFromFile();
}
```

In addition to the commonly used logical operators as shown in Table 2.4, there are the operators to join a number of statements together known as conditional operators. In applied programming there are many occasions where more than one condition must be evaluated, and for this there are the AND, OR and NOT operators (Table 2.5).

To examine how the conditional operators work with the commonly used operators consider the following as shown in Example 2.7. A

Table 2.5   Conditional operators

Operator	Description
&&	AND
||	OR
!	NOT

program goes through a list of bonds and adds the symbol to the portfolio where the bond has a yield of less than 10% or does not have a currency of JPY and a maturity of more than 5 years.

Example 2.7: Conditional and logical operators
```
if (((Yield < 0.1)||!(CCY == "JPY"))&&(mat > 5)
  portfolio.Add(symbol));
```

2.1.5   Operator precedence

In C#, as in most other programming languages, the operators have different rules of precedence. These are that the comparative operators work from left to right while the assign operators are right to left.

Consider the expression in Example 2.8 where there is a mathematical operator and an assign operator. What the programmer is trying to achieve is to assign the results of the rate divided by the number of days to a variable yield.

Example 2.8: Operator precedence
```
double yield = rate / numberOfDays
```

The first operator that is performed is `rate / numberOfDays`, and the result is then assigned to the variable yield. This has worked because the operator precedence is such that the calculation operation is performed before the assign operator.

Now consider Example 2.9 where there are two mathematical operators; the order in which the divide or the multiply are performed is important to the result.

Example 2.9: Precedence of logical operators
```
double yield = rate / numberOfDays * 100
```

The mathematical operations are performed from left to right, with the calculation of `rate / numberOfDays` being executed before being multiplied by 100. In Example 2.10, the same calculation is done but this time the brackets take higher precedence, meaning that the number of days multiplied by 100 is done before the division.

Example 2.10: Precedence of logical operators with brackets
```
double yield = rate /(numberOfDays * 100)
```

The best way to perform complicated calculations is either to break the calculation down into a number of steps or surround the blocks with brackets; this reaps rewards when it comes to maintenance of the code.

In Example 2.11 the calculation shows a number of brackets that make the code easier to understand.

Example 2.11: Excerpt from the Black Scholes formula

```
d1 = (Math.Log(S / X) + (r + v * v / 2.0) * T) /
     (v * Math.Sqrt(T));
```

An even better way to understand the line of code would be to break the formula down into smaller parts. This has the added advantage of being able to debug the individual lines and thus know what the interim values are. Example 2.12 shows how the line of code from Example 2.11 could be simplified for debugging.

Example 2.12: Excerpt from the Black Scholes formula broken down into smaller parts

```
L = Math.Log(S/X);
rv = r + v * v / 2.0;
sq = v * Math.Sqrt(T);
d1 = (L + rv * T)/sq;
```

Table 2.6 illustrates the ranking of operators in precedence with one being ranked the highest.

Table 2.6 does not contain the complete list of operators, as there are a number of operators that are seldom used in finance applications. For a complete list refer to either MSDN or a C# reference manual.

Table 2.6   Operator precedence ranked

Rank	Category	Operator
1	Primary	(x) $a[x]$ x++ x-
2	Unary	+ - ++x --x
3	Multiplicative	* / %
4	Additive	+ -
5	Shift	>> <<
6	Relational	<= < > >=
7	Equality	== !=
8	Conditional AND	&&
9	Conditional OR	||
10	Conditional	?:
11	Assignment	= += -= *= /=

2.2   DATA STRUCTURES

C# is a strongly typed language, meaning that all variables used must be declared. If a variable is initialised but not declared a compilation error will occur. In Example 2.13, the variable yield is assigned to without having been declared.

Example 2.13: A variable not being declared leads to a compile error
```
yield = 0;
```

```
The name 'yield' does not exist in the class or
namespace 'TradingApplication.PositionModelHandler'
```

In C# there are a wide variety of types to represent data; in this section data structures will be examined.

2.2.1   Built-in types

Built-in types in C# are aliases of predefined types. For example, bool is an alias of System.Boolean.

All the built-in types with the exception of string and object are known as simple types; string and object are known as built-in reference types. The built-in types and their alias may be used interchangeably as is seen in Example 2.14.

Example 2.14: Built-in types and their alias used interchangeably
```
String myvar = "hello world";
string myvar = "hello world";
```

string as a built-in reference type has a number of methods and properties that are explored later in this section, whereas a simple built-in type such as int has a very limited set of methods.

2.2.2   Casting and type converting

As C# is a strongly typed language, it is important that the data passed around are correctly assigned or converted, otherwise it will lead to a series of compile errors.

C# does lots of implicit conversions, such that a double may be converted to a string, as seen in Example 2.15 where quantity is declared a double but is implicitly converted to a string to pass into the Console.Write.

Example 2.15: Implicit conversion of a double to a string

```
Console.Write(" Quantity " + quantity + " adjusted by "
+ qty);
```

Explicit casting is done by including the type in brackets before the returning value. In Example 2.16 the explicit cast is done to ensure that a double returned from a dataset is assigned to a double.

Example 2.16: Explicit casting a double

```
double _price = (double)dr["price"];
```

If the explicit cast in Example 2.16 were omitted it would result in a compile error `Cannot implicitly convert type 'object' to 'double'`.

While C# can perform a variety of implicit and explicit casts there are situations where this is not possible. This is likely to happen when trying to convert a string value to a numeric value. As show in Example 2.17, when trying to assign a value from a text box on a Windows form to a numeric value, a conversion is needed. The first step is to ensure the `Text` value is a string by calling the `ToString` method and then using the `Parse` method in the `Double` class to convert the data to a double.

Example 2.17: Data conversion from a string to a double

```
if(this.txtQuantity.Text.ToString().Length > 0)
{
  qty = Double.Parse(this.txtQuantity.Text
.ToString());
}
```

The commonly used numeric classes `Decimal`, `Double`, `Single` and `Int32` all have a `Parse` method.

`DateTime` also includes a `Parse` method to convert the string representation of a date into a `DateTime` equivalent.

2.2.3 Strings

As in other OO languages a string is an object and has a number of methods and properties associated with it. Confusingly `String` and `string` are one and the same thing, `string` being an alias for `String`.

Example 2.18 shows a string being declared and a string being both declared and assigned to.

Example 2.18: Declaring and initialising string variables
```
private string _symbol;
string baseCCY_ = "EUR";
```

The sections that follow cover some of the ways to manipulate string data; not all of the sections covered are methods contained within the string class but are included as they are relevant to manipulating text data.

Matching strings

There are a number of ways of comparing strings in C#, the methods of Equal and CompareTo compare the string objects and the Unicode numbers of chars respectively, but the way to compare the string values is to use the equality (==) operator.

The safest way to compare two strings, if the case is not important, is to convert the two strings to either upper or lower case and use the equality operator to compare the values. In Example 2.19 the CallPutFlag is converted to lower case and the value compared to lower case "c".

Example 2.19: Converting strings to lower case to compare the values
```
if(CallPutFlag.ToLower() == "c")
{
  dBlackScholes = S * CumulativeNormalDistribution(d1)
  - X * Math.Exp(-r * T) *
  CumulativeNormalDistribution(d2);
}
```

Substring

```
string.Substring(start position, length)
```

There are times where extracting part values of a string is needed in a program. The method needs a starting position of the string and the length of the sub-string; if length is not given then it defaults to the end of the string.

An example of this would be extracting the first letter of a put or call type from a database retrieve as shown in Example 2.20. The letter is used as an internal flag in the OptionsPrice class.

Example 2.20: Extracting the first letter of the put/call type
```
dr["putCall"].ToString()).Substring(0,1).ToLower()
```

2.2.4 `StringBuilder`

As the string object is immutable, each time the contents are modified a new string object is created and returned. Where strings need concatenating, it is much more efficient to use the `StringBuilder` class.

In the error validation method illustrated in Example 2.21 the potential for a number of strings being concatenated is high, especially if the user hits enter by accident and submits a trade to be booked before completing the required fields. In this case the error messages are appended to a `StringBuilder` as each condition is validated. At the end of the method if any of the validations fail then the error message is created by calling the `ToString` method of the `StringBuilder` and an exception is thrown. Exceptions are covered in Chapter 3.

Example 2.21: `StringBuilder` being used to build a string of error messages
```
private void performValidations()
{
  Boolean err = false;
  StringBuilder msg = new StringBuilder();
  msg.Append("Validation error has occurred \n:");
  //Check trading Account
  if (_tacct.Length == 0)
  {
    msg.Append("Blank Trading account - mandatory
      field\n");
    err = true;
  }
  // Check customer account
  if(_custacct.Length == 0)
  {
    msg.Append("Blank Customer account - mandatory
      field \n");
    err = true;
  }
  // Check quantity
  if (_qty < 0)
  {
```

```
      msg.Append("Cannot have a negative quantity, use
        buy or sell to correct \n");
      err = true;
    }
    if(_bs.Length == 0)
    {
      msg.Append("Must be either a buy or sell\n");
      err = true;
    }
    if(_symbol.Length == 0)
    {
      msg.Append("Symbol is required - mandatory field
        \n");
      err = true;
    }
    if (err)
    {
      throw new TradeException(msg.ToString());
    }
}
```

The StringBuilder constructor has a number of overload constructors to initialise the capacity of the StringBuilder. By initialising the capacity it makes the appending of data more efficient as the StringBuilder object is not having to re-allocate space. Capacity is the property that contains the capacity of the StringBuilder, and the method EnsureCapacity may also be used to ensure that the StringBuilder has the minimum capacity of the value given. Unless size is very important the StringBuilder class seems to handle the 'growth' of its capacity efficiently.

StringBuilder comes with a range of methods, to append, remove and replace characters from the instance. The method most widely used is Append to append data to the end of the instance; the data that can be appended are either text or numeric types.

2.2.5 Regex

The Regular expression is included here as a string-related class that is a very powerful way of pattern matching and manipulating strings. The regular expressions are compatible with those in Perl 5.

A simple demonstration of Regex is shown in Example 2.22. A comma-separated file is read and the values need extracting into an array. The Regular Expression instance is initialised with the regular expression, in this case a comma. When the file is read, each line is examined and using the Split method the values returned into an array. The array in this example is then appended to a hashtable.

Example 2.22: String manipulation using regular expressions
```
Regex rExp = new Regex(",");
StreamReader sIn = new StreamReader(_path,true);
string line;
  do
  {
    line = sIn.ReadLine();
    if (line != null)
    {
      string[] ccFX = rExp.Split(line);
      _rates.Add(ccFX[0],ccFX[1]);
    }
  } while (line != null);
```

2.2.6 Arrays

Arrays in C# are objects that are indexed. The indexing in C# is zero-based, thus Array[0] is the first index reference in an array.

Initialising arrays

The declaration and initialisation either has an array size in square brackets, or uses a series of values enclosed in {} brackets.

Example 2.23: Initialising arrays
```
string[] categories = new string[3];
string[] categories = {"trading","cust","hedge"};
```

The square brackets [] denote the type as being an array. Thus any object type can have an array and the associated methods. Accessing a simple array is done by referencing the element number array[int], or by item array["item"].

Multiple dimension arrays

Adding a comma to the square brackets in a single-dimensioned array declaration introduces dimensions to the array. Example 2.24 shows a two-dimensional array being declared to hold a 20 by 2 array.

Example 2.24: Multiple dimensioned array
```
double[,] deltaValue = new double[20,2];
```

  The other way is to declare a multiple-dimension array as an array of arrays (as opposed to the matrix example of the above). Example 2.25 shows two arrays being assigned to an array of arrays.

Example 2.25: An array of arrays being declared and initialised
```
double[][] priceArray = new double[2][];
priceArray[0] = new double[]{101.25,98.75,100.50};
priceArray[1] = new double[]{101.25,102.0};
```

To reference the elements of a multiple-dimension array, the comma is used in the brackets with row followed by column:

```
array[row,column]
```

Array methods and properties

When working with arrays the most frequently used property is the Length property. This gives the number of elements of the array, making the iteration through the array possible. Example 2.26 shows how an array is iterated through with Length being the array capacity.

Example 2.26: Iterating through an array
```
for (int i=0;i<categories.Length;i++)
{
   loadFromDB(categories[i]);
}
```

Arrays have the GetEnumerator method, which returns an IEnumerator from the System.Collections namespace. This gives the flexibility of using the enumerator methods to access the array, such as the GetNext methods.
  Enumerators and collections will be discussed in the next section.

2.2.7   Collections

Collections are a set of objects grouped together; C# is no different to other languages in providing interfaces for collections, such as enumerating, comparing, and creating collections.

IEnumerable interface contains only the method GetEnumerator, the purpose of which is to return an IEnumerator.

Collections such as arrays or hashtables in turn implement the GetEnumerator method that returns an IEnumerator.

The GetEnumerator method passing an IEnumerator is used in Example 2.27 to return a collection of foreign exchange rates; these are then iterated through using the MoveNext method and the values extracted using the Current property.

Example 2.27: An enumerator being returned and being used

```
private string[] getFXlist()
{
  IEnumerator fx = _rates.GetEnumerator();
  string[] fxrtn = new string[_rates.Count];
  int i = 0;
  while(fx.MoveNext())
  {
    fxrtn[i++] = (string)fx.Current;
  }
  return fxrtn;
}
```

MoveNext() returns a Boolean that returns false when there are no more items to return. The Current property returns the current element in the collection.

ArrayLists

ArrayLists are very useful when you do not know how many elements you have, and offer the functionality of the usual fixed size array. Rather than assigning an array with more elements than expected and trapping any overflow errors the ArrayList size can dynamically grow.

There are a number of important methods; Add lets you dynamically add to the ArrayList, the Capacity property is used to either set the number of elements of the ArrayList or it returns the number of elements, and finally there is GetEnumerator that returns an enumerator.

The ArrayList is used in the ConnectionPool where an initial number of connections to a database are created. If all the connections are in use it is important to be able to create a new connection and manage it in the pool. The ConnectionPool example (Example 4.10) shows the ArrayList in use.

Hashtables

Hashtables are similar to Hashtables in Java, and Perl. They are used to store paired values, with a key and a value, and offer a more flexible way of accessing data from a collection.

The values can be any object, such as objects, Hashtables or strings. The trick with Hashtables is having simple keys to extract or manipulate the values.

C# provides access to the values by using the item property as shown in Example 2.28, because Hashtable implements the IDictionary interface.

Example 2.28: Accessing a Hashtable using an item
```
fxTable["EUR"]
```

In Example 2.29 the Hashtable returns an IDictionary Enumerator which is a special type of IEnumerator that is a read only implementation with the properties of Key and Value returning the dictionary keys and values.

Example 2.29: Hashtable returning an IDictionaryEnumerator in order to iterate through the Hashtable.
```
FX fxOb = new FX();
Hashtable fxT = (Hashtable)fxOb.getRatesHash();
IDictionaryEnumerator fxE = fxT.GetEnumerator();
while (fxE.MoveNext())
{
    this.lstFX.Items.Add(fxE.Key + " \t " + fxE.Value);
}
```

As shown in Example 2.28 the Add method is an important method to build a Hashtable, in addition the Delete method is used to remove an entry from a Hashtable, and `Clear` removes all the elements from the Hashtable.

2.3   CONTROL STRUCTURES

Having covered the data types and the common operators this section ties the two aspects together. C# features all conditional statements and loop controls that are central to writing applications. This section will cover the common structures and show examples where applicable.

2.3.1   if/else

if (condition) [{] statement [}else {statement }]

The condition tested is in brackets, with the next block executed. You may use braces {} if there are several lines of code that need executing.

In Example 2.30 the test is made on the variable X to see if it is greater than zero; if so the cumulative normal distribution is subtracted from one before being returned, otherwise it is returned as is.

Example 2.30: An `if/else` example
```
if (X < 0)
{
   return 1.0 - dCND;
}
else
{
   return dCND;
}
```

Note the braces {} can be ignored if a single statement follows an `if` statement, such as the code shown in Example 2.31.

Example 2.31: An `if` statement being used without braces
```
if (ds != null)
   ((DataGrid)_objectCollection["grid"]).DataSource =
   ds.Tables[0].DefaultView;
```

In practice including the braces {} improves the readability of the code.

2.3.2 `switch`

switch (variable or statement)

```
{
    case value:
        code body;
        exit statement;
   [default:
        code body;
        exit statement;]
}
```

`switch` is used where there are a number of conditions that need evaluating and it takes the pain out of lots of nested `if`/`else` statements. However, `switch` may only be used to evaluate a number of decisions based on integral or string types.

In Example 2.32 the account category is being evaluated and depending on the category the appropriate SQL statement is being generated; note in this example there is no default case being used.

Example 2.32: `switch` statement used to evaluate the account category

```
switch (category)
{
  case "positions":
    sql = positionsCategory(category);
    break;
  case "hedge":
    sql = positionsCategory(category);
    break;
  case "trades":
    sql = getTrades();
    break
}
```

2.3.3 `while`

while (condition) {code body}

By using the `while` statement, as long as the condition remains true the program will loop around the code body. The loop condition is evaluated before the code body has executed. In Example 2.33 `while` is used with an enumerator with the `MoveNext` method, which will return true until there are no more records to be processed.

Example 2.33: `while` loop shown in context of an enumerator

```
while (fxE.MoveNext())
{
   this.lstFX.Items.Add(fxE.Key + "\t " + fxE.Value);
}
```

2.3.4 `do/while`

do {code body} while (condition)

`do/while` is similar to `while`, the big difference being in evaluating the condition. In `do/while` the condition is examined after the code body in the loop has run, whereas `while` evaluates the condition before looping.

In Example 2.34 a file is being read until the line returned is `null`; note that the `ReadLine` is executed before the check that line is null.

Example 2.34: `do/while` loop evaluating the line after the loop being processed

```
do
{
   line = sIn.ReadLine();
   if (line != null)
   {
     string[] ccFX = rExp.Split(line);
     _rates.Add(ccFX[0],ccFX[1]);
   }
}
 while (line != null);
```

2.3.5 `for` loop

for (initialise counter; exit condition; counter) {code body}

The block of code in a `for` loop iterates around with the counter being initialised, the condition checking and the counter all being on the same line.

In Example 2.35 the `for` loop begins at zero and loops around until the condition `I<_initialPool` is met; the example shows the `for` loop used in initialising a number of database connections.

Example 2.35: For loop showing a number of connections being initialised

```
private void initConnections()
{
    for(int i=0;i<_initialPool;i++)
    {
        addConnection(i);
    }
}
```

2.3.6 `foreach` loop

```
foreach (element in collection)
{
    code body;
}
```

The `foreach` loop is used to iterate through either collections or arrays, and goes through each element until the last one is reached. In writing a `foreach` loop, the structure of the collection should remain unchanged otherwise the loop could cause some unpredictable results. Example 2.36 shows a collection being created and the elements being iterated through. The example is taken from a class that builds a dynamic string of SQL.

Example 2.36: `foreach` loop being used to iterate through a collection to build a dynamic SQL query

```
ICollection keys = hashFields.Keys;
foreach(string key in keys)
{
    field.Append(key);
    field.Append(",");
}
```

2.4 SUMMARY

This section has dealt with the basics of programming in C#, covering operators, data types and how they fit in with control structures.

Operators cover a variety of functionality. At the most simple there are the assignment operator and the common mathematical operators. There are also the operators that perform a mathematical operation and assign the result, and the special prefix and postfix operators used in incrementing and decrementing values in an integer by one. The logical operators are widely used in control structures where there are conditional statements, and are often used with conditional operators to join them together.

Taking all the operators together the order of precedence was looked at from the point of understanding which operators are ranked higher and how this impacts the results. In looking at precedence, the importance of brackets and breaking down complicated calculations as good practice was emphasised, allowing code to be read more easily and making debugging simpler.

C# is a strongly typed language like C++ and Java. There are a number of built-in types that are aliased to the classes in the system workspace as the core of C#. Casting and type converting were examined, as there are frequently cases where data need moving and objects may return data as different types. Numeric data have the `Parse` method to help parse text data into numeric data; this is widely used where data are captured in Window forms.

`string` and `StringBuilder` are ways of containing string data and the various methods were examined. It is important when to use `string` and `StringBuilder` as `string` is immutable while `StringBuilder` is mutable.

In looking at string manipulation, the use of regular expressions was discussed with the `Regex` class.

Arrays and collections were examined as a useful set of data types widely used in programs. The distinction between `Arrays` and `ArrayLists` was discussed. With collections the importance of enumerators was examined as a means of iterating through collections and how to access the data within the iteration loop.

Having looked at the operators and data types, the control structures were introduced. This showed how the operators and data types are applied in these structures as well as introducing the structures themselves.

Armed with the basics of C#, the more powerful aspects of it are now examined with application to financial software.

3

Object Oriented Programming

The most powerful aspect of C# is the Object Oriented features and in this section you will explore these features and how they are applied to a financial application. The Object Oriented concepts are illustrated with code taken from a small futures and options application sample. The Windows application was written from a practical perspective to demonstrate the various concepts covered from the viewpoint of a derivatives application. The full source code is available to download at http://www.wileyeurope.com/go/worner.

Programmers learning C# in finance will perhaps have backgrounds in C++, Java or Visual Basic. Perhaps the understanding of objects and classes is a given to most developers, even so a quick overview may be beneficial before getting into the details of Object Oriented programming in C# applied to finance.

A class is a description of an object; it describes the properties and the methods that are encapsulated within it. An object in the programming world is an entity that contains properties and has some defined behaviour known as methods.

A class becomes an object when it is instantiated; a class cannot be accessed directly, it must be declared and initialised.

The real power of classes is that the logic is encapsulated and may be extended, reused. C# has a large range of in-built classes which means that the developer can begin building the business logic without having to develop a large toolkit to support Windows applications.

3.1 INTRODUCTION TO CLASSES

[attributes] [modifiers (access)] class identifier
[: list of base classes and/or interfaces]{}

There are a number of basic requirements for creating a class; Example 3.1 shows how a simple class is declared.

Example 3.1: A simple class declaration
```
using System;
{
```

```
public class LogError
{
// . . .
}
}
```

The first step is to include any references needed in the class; in C# these are referred to as assemblies. The references are actually DLL, EXE or project files that are linked to the working project. The keyword using followed by the reference name is the way to include them; in Example 3.2 the system reference with the basic classes and the references to the Data, Text, and Odbc classes are included.

Example 3.2: Reference declarations
```
using System;
using System.Data;
using System.Text;
using Microsoft.Data.Odbc;
```

In addition to the references, C# has the concept of grouping classes and interfaces into namespaces. This grouping means that the classes and public properties are available to one another within the namespace. Note that if a project is created with no namespace then a default one gets created anyway.

Looking at how the class is constructed in Example 3.1, the class is defined with a modifier type, in this case public. The allowable access modifiers for a class are either public or internal. Public means that the class is accessible to all assemblies, internal is accessible only to the files within the assembly to which the class belongs.

Then comes the keyword class followed by the class name (in Example 3.1 this is LogError) and the braces {} are set to denote the scope of the class.

In creating a class, the next step is to define a constructor, some methods and properties where applicable. The constructor is how the object is called when it is being instantiated. Example 3.3 shows how the LogError class is instantiated and the parameter e passed as the constructor specifies.

Example 3.3: LogError class instantiated with the parameter being passed as defined by the constructor
```
LogError eL = new LogError(e);
```

In declaring the constructor it must have the same name as the class; if one is not declared then the default constructor is created by the compiler with no arguments and no code to execute, as Example 3.4 shows.

Example 3.4: Default constructor

```
public LogError()
{
}
```

In Example 3.5 there are two constructors; this is known as constructor overloading. Overloading is used where there may be a number of different arguments to call the same object; in this case the LogError is created with either an exception or a string.

Constructor overloading comes into its own when a core class needs modifying in the way it is called; rather than change every class that references, a new constructor is written.

Example 3.5: Constructor overloading

```
public LogError(Exception e)
{
 Console.WriteLine(e.StackTrace);
 Console.WriteLine(e.Message);
}
public LogError(string err)
{
 Console.WriteLine(err);
}
```

Example 3.6 shows how the LogError object is created with the different constructors, one having a string passed, the other an exception.

Example 3.6: Having overloaded constructors shows how the LogError class can be called with different arguments

```
String eMsg = "Error Message";
LogError eL2 = new LogError(eMsg);

catch (System.DivideByZeroException e)
{
 LogError eL = new LogError(e);
}
```

In addition to the constructor, it is possible to initialise some variables as the object is created. In Example 3.7 the instance variable _r is created and assigned a value as the object is created. It has been given the keyword const to indicate that the value may not change; the other variables have been declared but not initialised and may be modified. Initialising a variable at the object's creation is useful for setting default values, which may be overridden as part of the class behaviour.

Example 3.7: Initialised instance variable _r is created and assigned a value with the object

```
public class OptionsPrice : Iprice
{
// declare private variables
private const double _r = 0.04; // risk free
rate
private double _S; // Stock price
private double _T; // Days to expiry
private double _X; // Strike
private double _v; // volatility
private string _callPut;
private string _symb;
```

The next stage in creating a class is to give it some behaviour. Setting the behaviour of a class is done by adding methods. A method is a means for a class to define some behaviour.

[modifiers (access)] return-type name (parameters) { }

At a minimum, a method must have a return type declared, or be void if nothing is returned, and a method name. In Example 3.8 a method getPrice is declared; it takes no parameter arguments, it calls another method with some instance variables and returns a double. Note if the return type is not void then the keyword return is required with the correct return type. The data type can be any valid built-in type or a defined type within the project; this may be either an object in the project or an object in a referenced assembly.

Example 3.8: The getPrice method that takes no parameter arguments and returns a double

```
public double getPrice()
{
_price = BlackScholes(_callPut,_S,_X,_T,_r,_v);
return _price;
}
```

Table 3.1 Access modifiers in methods

Access type	Description
public	visible by all classes
private	only available within the class
protected	accessible to the class and to classes derived from the class
internal	accessible to the current project

Example 3.8 was declared with the access type as public. Table 3.1 shows the other access types and what they mean.

Example 3.9 shows an example of a method that is declared with a number of parameters; this is then called as shown in Example 3.8.

Example 3.9: A method with a list of parameters declared

```
private double BlackScholes(string CallPutFlag, double
 S,double X,double T, double r, double v)
```

Parameters are passed by value by default; to pass by reference the keywords `ref` or `out` are used. The difference in passing by value and by reference is that when a variable is passed as a parameter by value a copy is being passed and it can be changed within the object without the variable in the calling method being changed. The `ref` keyword means that the parameter is passed by reference so that any changes that occur to the parameter within the program will be reflected in the calling method and the variable. The `out` keyword is very similar to `ref` only in that the variable must be declared and initialised when used in conjunction with `ref`, whereas `out` does not need the variable initialised.

There are some performance improvements if large objects are passed by reference, thus avoiding creating a copy of the large object. However, it may be clearer in the code to have `getter` and `setter` methods or properties to return the data rather than 'by reference' updating.

Example 3.10: A class with two methods that pass by value and reference respectively

```
public class ValueAndReference
{
 public ValueAndReference()
  {
  }
  public float getInterestByVal(float coupon,
   float days,float months)
```

```
{
float result = coupon * months / days;
days = 365;
months = 15;
return result;
}
public float getInterestByRef(ref float
  coupon,ref float days,ref float months)
{
float result = coupon * months / days;
days = 365;
months = 15;
return result;

}

}

private void doSomething()
{
 float coupon = 0.033F;
 float days = 360F;
 float months = 30F;

  ValueAndReference T = new ValueAndReference();
  float intVal = T.getInterestByVal(coupon,days,months);
  Console.WriteLine("Coupon = " + coupon + " Days = "
   + days + " months = " + months);
  float intRef = T.getInterestByRef(ref coupon,ref
   days,ref months);
  Console.WriteLine("Coupon = " + coupon + " Days = "
   + days + " months = " + months);
}
```

Output:

```
Coupon = 0.033 Days = 360 months = 30
Coupon = 0.033 Days = 365 months = 15
```

The other important feature of a class is being able to define proper-ties; this encapsulates the class data. Properties are ways of setting and retrieving data, and they may be defined independently to set and return data.

Example 3.11 shows the property name with a `getter` and `setter` type being declared.

Example 3.11: Property symbol with get and set declared

```
public string symbol
{
  get{ return (string)_derivAttrib["symbol"]; }
  set{ _derivAttrib["symbol"] = value;}
}
```

Accessing the property is shown in Example 3.12; it is assigned to or returned from like an instance variable.

Example 3.12: Working with the symbol property

```
Option o = new Option();
o.symbol = _symb;
Console.Write("Symbol set to : " + o.symbol);
```

This is a shortened way of creating a `get` and `set` method to set and retrieve data. Example 3.12 shows a simplistic property; the set method would usually have some data validation steps to ensure data integrity.

The alternative to properties is to write a `get` and `set` method; this would be accessed as a regular method when called.

The basics of writing a class have now been covered. Later in this chapter, we will explore how classes fit together with inheritance and polymorphism and how it is applied to finance.

3.1.1   Exception handling

```
try
{
}
catch(Exception e)
{
}
finally
{
}
```

In all applications the ability to handle exceptions is fundamental, as there are circumstances in a program when the 'unexpected' happens. In C# there are a wide variety of built-in system exceptions; in addition, exception classes can be written to handle specific errors.

An exception is handled in a try/catch block. The try block around a block of code denotes the code where the exception is being handled. The catch keyword is used with the braces {} to handle the exception. The catch statement may be used to handle as many exceptions as are required, for example there may be a need to handle divide by zero exceptions, and in the case of numeric overflow two catch statements are required.

In addition to catch there is the finally keyword, the purpose of which is to execute the block of code regardless of whether there has been an exception or not. The finally block is useful, for example, in closing open database connections or files.

In Example 3.13 the try/catch blocks handle database errors; note in this example that the finally statement is always called to release the connection back to the pool.

Example 3.13: try block around a database and a catch block to handle errors

```
public DataSet dbSelect(string sqlstr)
{
 ConnectPool c = ConnectPool.GetInstance();
 OdbcConnection con = c.getConnection();
 DataSet DSet = new DataSet();
 try
 {
  _dbAdapter.SelectCommand = con.CreateCommand();
  _dbAdapter.SelectCommand.CommandText = sqlstr;
  _dbAdapter.Fill(DSet);
 }
 catch (OdbcException dbE)
 {
 LogError eLog = new LogError(dbE);
 eLog.writeErr(sqlstr);
 DSet = null;
 }
 finally
 {
 c.releaseConnection();
```

```
}
    return DSet;
}
```

3.1.2   User defined exception class

In addition to the wealth of exception classes there are times when a customised error needs to be generated and caught to deal with a specific set of conditions.

In the futures and options application there is a trade booking section; before a trade is booked there is a check to ensure that the mandatory fields are completed. If any of the mandatory field values are missing then an exception needs throwing to alert the user that there are missing fields. In generating the exception the keyword throw is used.

Note the user defined exception classes derive from the ApplicationException and NOT the SystemException class. The three constructors shown in Example 3.14 must be present in user-defined exceptions.

In Example 3.14 the exception is a very simple implementation of a user defined exception class using the functionality of the base class ApplicationException.

Example 3.14: User defined exception class, TradeException

```
public class TradeException : System.Application
    Exception
{
    // Default constructor
    public TradeException() : base("Trade Exception
     Thrown")
    {
    }
    // Custom constructor that receives a string
    public TradeException(string msg) : base(msg)
    {
    }
    // Constructor that receives string and Exception
    public TradeException(string message,Exception exp)
     : base(message,exp)
    {
    }
}
```

Example 3.15 shows how the TradeException is thrown if one of the checks are not met.

Example 3.15: Throwing a TradeException

```
private void performValidations()
{
 Boolean err = false;
 StringBuilder msg = new StringBuilder();
 msg.Append("Validation error has occurred:");
 // Check trading Account
 if (_tacct.Length == 0)
 {
  msg.Append("Blank Trading account - mandatory
   field \n");
    err = true;
 }
 // Check customer account
 if(_custacct.Length == 0)
 {
 msg.Append("Blank Customer account - mandatory
  field \n");
   err = true;
 }
 // Check quantity
 if (_qty < 0)
 {
 msg.Append("Cannot have a negative quantity, use
  buy or sell to correct \n");
   err = true;
 }
 if(_bs.Length == 0)
 {
   msg.Append("Must have either a buy or sell\n");
   err = true;
 }
 if(_symbol.Length == 0)
 {
   msg.Append("Symbol is required - mandatory
     field \n");
   err = true;
 }
```

```
if (err)
{
   throw new TradeException(msg.ToString());
}
}
```

Example 3.16 shows how the TradeException is handled on the form with the exception being caught using the try and catch blocks.

Example 3.16: User defined Exception TradeException being handled in a block of code

```
try
{
   Trade tr = new Trade(tacct,custacct,qty,price,bs,
      symbol,ccy,fx);
}
catch (TradeException except)
{
   MessageBox.Show(except.Message);
}
finally
{
   // Refresh the grids
   pHandler.reloadData("all");
   // Clear the input box
   clearFields();
}
```

3.1.3   Workshop: Exercise one

This workshop is the first in a series of workshops that are built on throughout the book. The idea is that by building on the workshops the end result is a relevant application; an options calculator was chosen for its simplicity in terms of building an application. Each workshop takes the application a step further as well as giving you the chance to put into practice some of the concepts you have just learnt.

The specification has been written and can be found in Appendix A; in addition, a diagrammatic representation of the options calculator can be seen in Appendix B. The actual models implemented in creating the workshops can be seen in Appendix C, along with details of how to download the source files.

The first part of the workshop is to create a new Windows application project. By default a Windows form is added to the project. Add the following components on the form.

Text boxes and labels
   Strike price
   Stock Price
   Volatility
   Risk Free rate
   Result (set to read-only and use it to display the price).
DateTime Picker
   Expiry Date
Radio buttons
   Put and call
   Black Scholes and Implicit Finite-Difference
Button
   Calculate

These form the input boxes required by the models to return a price. Further components will be added onto the form as the exercises progress through the book.

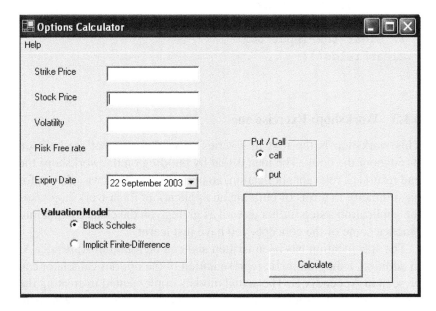

Figure 3.1 Basic options calculation form

Create a new class that will encapsulate these input fields called option. Overload the constructor so that the constructor can take the input parameters from the form as either text data directly from the form text boxes or numeric data where the data have already been converted to numeric data where applicable. Create the input parameters as read-only properties.

For this exercise create a method called getMessage which returns a string.

The final step is to add the event onclick to the calculate button, and then in the code block create an option object passing the parameters collected from the form. Call the getMessage method putting the output to a MessageBox.

Try running the project, entering some values and clicking the calculate button. If it all compiles and runs, the result of clicking the calculate button should be a pop-up message returning the string from getMessage.

You may have noticed that a system exception occurs if no values are entered into the text boxes. There should be some validation in place to trap the errors and inform the users that an error has occurred and what steps they need to take to correct it.

At the absolute minimum some try/catch blocks need putting around the parsing of the text to a numeric field. The better approach is to perform the numeric parse in the option class and throw an OptionException, catching it in the form. OptionException is not a system exception and will need writing.

As we have learnt, an application exception must have the three constructors created to handle the various ways. Create a new class and name it OptionException; base it around Example 3.14.

In the option class, where the numeric parsing is done, add some validation. If there are any validation errors then an OptionException needs throwing.

In the form class, place a try/catch block around the option object to catch the OptionException and in the catch block alert the user to the validation error, as shown in Figure 3.2.

3.2 INHERITANCE AND POLYMORPHISM

In C#, as in other Object Oriented languages, the ability to inherit from other classes and interfaces introduces program reuse from a practical approach. The methods and properties of one class can be used by other classes that inherit from it. What this means in applied programming is

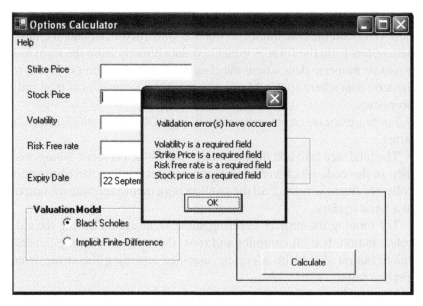

Figure 3.2   Validation error

that a set of common features are built into a base class and the specific elements of functionality are built into the inherited class.

There are cases where each of the derived classes will need to have their own customised method where the base class method is overridden. This is known as polymorphism.

In the next section the application of inheritance and polymorphism through base classes and interfaces is explored. An example will be looked at through design to implementation. Note in C# that it is only possible to inherit from one base class, otherwise known as single inheritance.

3.2.1   Applying inheritance and polymorphism to finance

The best way to understand how inheritance and polymorphism are applied is to work through an example.

While derivative products have a number of shared attributes and behaviour there are some features specific to each product.

In the futures and options trading application, the futures and options products are encapsulated into objects to hold the data needed and provide methods to incorporate their behaviour.

There are several approaches to this. A class can written for each product type encapsulating the properties and methods; the downside of this approach is that there are common behaviours and properties that would be duplicated in each class.

A better way is by using inheritance, and polymorphism. Looking at a future and an option in detail we can compare the features of each product and create a grid of common features and specific properties and behaviour. As seen in Table 3.2 there is much in common with the two types of derivatives and some specific properties unique to the instrument.

In designing the product classes a base class is created to encapsulate the common properties and methods; the Future and Option classes inherit the base class and then are extended to encapsulate the specific properties of each product.

Futures and options may share many attributes, but they do have some specific data that are peculiar to the product type. Thus the base class will have a method to retrieve the common data from the database and supply a method to load the product specific data required by both the Future and Option class. This then allows the Futures and Options classes to implement their specific retrieval, thus exhibiting polymorphic behaviour.

The Add to Database, addToDB, method can be defined in the base class and written in such a way that it can handle the insertion to the product tables for both products.

Table 3.3 shows the relationship between the base class and the Future and Option classes. The base class Derivative contains the common properties and methods. The Option and Future classes contain their own implementation of the loadExtrasFromDB method, which loads product-specific properties from the database.

Table 3.2 Comparison of the properties and behaviour of a Future and an Option

Property/behaviour	Future	Option
Name	x	x
Days to expiry	x	x
Strike price	x	x
Symbol	x	x
Underlying price	x	x
Underlying symbol	x	x
Delta	x	x
Contract size	x	
Put or Call		x
US or Euro style		x
Volatility		x
Add to database	x	x
Retrieve from database	x	x

Table 3.3 A representation of the base class `Derivative` and the classes `Option` and `Future` that inherit from them

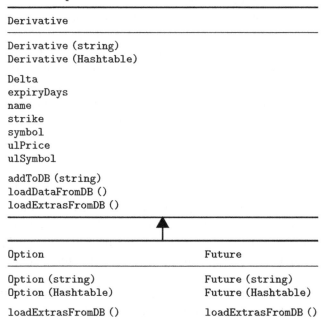

```
Derivative
```
```
Derivative (string)
Derivative (Hashtable)
```
```
Delta
expiryDays
name
strike
symbol
ulPrice
ulSymbol
```
```
addToDB (string)
loadDataFromDB ()
loadExtrasFromDB ()
```

Option	Future
Option (string)	Future (string)
Option (Hashtable)	Future (Hashtable)
loadExtrasFromDB ()	loadExtrasFromDB ()

Having looked at how to approach the creation of the objects and the relationship between them we will now examine how it is done in C#.

Declaring the `Derivative` class as an abstract class means that the class cannot be instantiated directly and may only be used as a base class. Example 3.17 shows how the class is declared abstract.

Example 3.17: Abstract class declaration
```
public abstract class Derivative
{
}
```

The next step is to declare a `Hashtable` to hold the data as shown in Example 3.18; in a simple class this would be held in a private instance variable. As this is a base class this variable must be visible in the inherited classes and is thus declared protected, which means it cannot be accessed outside the derived class.

Example 3.18: Declaring a protected `Hashtable` to make it accessible in `Option` and `Future`
```
// Declare private variables
protected Hashtable_derivAttrib = new Hashtable();
```

The method loadExtrasFromDB() is implemented differently in the Future and Option classes to accommodate the different attributes of these products. The ability to implement different functionality in the same method is known as overriding. The method is declared as virtual, as illustrated in Example 3.19 to allow overriding. This must be done as all methods are defaulted to non-virtual and thus may not be overridden.

Example 3.19: Creating a virtual method
```
protected virtual void loadExtrasFromDB(){}
```

The constructors and common properties are then created in the base class Derivative; this can be seen in Example 3.26 where a full listing of the Derivative, Option and Future classes is shown.

Having written the Derivative class the Option class must now be written. The class is declared with the colon followed by Derivative, as shown in Example 3.20, meaning that the class inherits from Derivative.

Example 3.20: Option inherits from Derivative
```
public class Option : Derivative
{
}
```

The next step is writing the constructors for the class Option. Inheriting from Derivative means that it must implement the same constructors as Derivative; note that Derivative did not have a default constructor. Example 3.21 shows the Option class declaring the two constructors, with the base keyword specifying that the base constructor be called when the object Option is instantiated.

Example 3.21: Declaring the constructors and specifying that the constructor in the base class be used
```
public Option(string symbol):base(symbol)
{
}
public Option(Hashtable h):base(h)
{
}
```

The loadExtrasFromDB method is overridden in the Option class, the override keyword indicating that the method is being overridden, thus displaying polymorphic behaviour. The extra fields are appended into the Hashtable that contains the class data.

Example 3.22: Overriding the loadExtrasFromDB method from the base class Derivative

```
protected override void loadExtrasFromDB()
{
 string sql = "select putCall,euroUSType from
 tblProduct where pSymbol = '" + base.symbol + "'";
 DBHandler db = new DBHandler();
 DataSet ds = db.dbSelect(sql);
 DataRow dr = ds.Tables[0].Rows[0];
 _derivAttrib.Add("putCall",(dr["putCall"].ToString())
  .Substring(0,1). ToLower());
 _derivAttrib.Add("usEuro",(dr["euroUSType"].ToString
 ()).Substring(0,1). ToLower());
}
```

The extra properties that are required for the Option are added in the usual way of declaring properties as shown in Example 3.23.

Example 3.23: Option specific properties

```
public string putCallType{ get {return (string)
 _derivAttrib["putCall"];}}
public string usEuro{ get {return (string)
 _derivAttrib["usEuro"];}}
```

The next class to be written is the Futures class which is similar in structure to the Options class as it derives the methods and properties from the base class Derivative. The big difference is the properties implemented and the overridden method loadExtrasFromDB. The Future class has the same implementation of the constructors using the keyword base.

Example 3.24: Future class derived from Derivative

```
public class Future : Derivative
{
 public Future(string symbol):base(symbol)
 {
 }
 public Future(Hashtable h):base(h)
```

```
{
}
public string contract{ get{return
  (string)_derivAttrib["contract"];}}

protected override void loadExtrasFromDB()
{
  string sql = "select contractSize from tblProduct
   where pSymbol = '" + base.symbol + "'";
  DBHandler db = new DBHandler();
  DataSet ds = db.dbSelect(sql);
  Console.Write(sql);
  DataRow dr = ds.Tables[0].Rows[0];
  _derivAttrib.Add("contract",(int)dr["contractSize"]);

}
}
```

Now both classes are built with the inherited methods and properties of the Derivative class. When the Option and Future objects are instantiated the properties and methods are available from both the base class of Derivative and the derived classes Option and Future. Example 3.25 shows the Option class being instantiated and the properties used.

Example 3.25: Option class being instantiated and the properties referenced
```
public void setParams(string symbol)
{
  _symb = symbol;
  Option o = new Option(_symb);
  _T = o.expiryDays;
  _X = o.strike;
  _callPut = o.putCallType;
  _S = o.ulPrice;
}
```

The full listing of the Derivative, Option and Future classes is shown in Example 3.26.

Example 3.26: The complete source code for the `Derivative`, `Option` and `Future` classes

```
public abstract class Derivative
{
 // Declare private variables
 protected Hashtable _derivAttrib = new Hashtable();
 //
 public Derivative(string _symbol)
 {
  symbol = _symbol;
  loadDataFromDB();
  loadExtrasFromDB();
 }
 public Derivative(Hashtable hashFields)
 {
  StringBuilder field = new StringBuilder();
  StringBuilder vals = new StringBuilder();
  StringBuilder sql = new StringBuilder();
  sql.Append("INSERT INTO tblProduct ");
  field.Append(" (");
  vals.Append(" VALUES (");
  ICollection keys = hashFields.Keys;
  ICollection values = hashFields.Values;
  foreach(string key in keys)
  {
   field.Append(key);
   field.Append(",");
  }
  field.Remove(field.Length - 1,1); // remove the
   last comma
  field.Append(")");
  foreach(string val in values)
  {
   vals.Append(val);
   vals.Append(",");
  }
  vals.Remove(vals.Length -1,1); // chop the last
   comma
  vals.Append(")");
  sql.Append(field.ToString());
  sql.Append(vals.ToString());
```

```
addToDB(sql.ToString());
}

public string name
{
  get{ return (string)_derivAttrib["name"];}
  set{_derivAttrib["name"] = value;}
}

public string symbol
{
  get{ return (string)_derivAttrib["symbol"]; }
  set{_derivAttrib["symbol"] = value;}
}
public string ulSymbol
{
  get {return (string)_derivAttrib["ul"];}
}
public double delta
{
  get {return (double)_derivAttrib["delta"];}
}
public double strike
{
  get
  {return (double)_derivAttrib["strike"];}
}

public double expiryDays
{
  get {return (double)_derivAttrib["expDays"];}
}
public double ulPrice
{
  get
  {return (double)_derivAttrib["ulPrice"];}
}

private void loadDataFromDB(){
    string sql = "select underlySymbol,delta,strike,
    expiry from tblProduct " + " where pSymbol ='" +
```

```
      (string)_derivAttrib["symbol"] + "'";
      DBHandler db = new DBHandler();
      DataSet ds = db.dbSelect(sql);
      DataRow dr = ds.Tables[0].Rows[0];
      DateTime expire = (DateTime)dr["expiry"];
      DateTime today = new DateTime();
      today = DateTime.Now;
      TimeSpan t = expire.Subtract(today);
      _derivAttrib.Add("ul",(string)dr["underlySymbol"]);
      _derivAttrib.Add("delta",(double)dr["delta"]);
      _derivAttrib.Add("strike",(double)dr["strike"]);
      _derivAttrib.Add("expDays",(double)t.TotalDays);
      // get the underlyer information
      sql = "select price from tblPrices where pSymbol =
      '" + (string)dr["underlySymbol"] + "'";
      ds = db.dbSelect(sql);
      if (ds.Tables[0].Rows.Count > 0)
      {
         dr = ds.Tables[0].Rows[0];
         _derivAttrib.Add("ulPrice",(double)dr["price"]);
   }
   else
   {
         _derivAttrib.Add("ulPrice",0.00);
   }
}
   private void addToDB(string sql)
   {
      DBHandler db = new DBHandler();
      string res = db.dbInsert(sql);
      if (res.Length>0)
      {
         LogError lErr = new LogError(res);
      }
   }
   protected virtual void loadExtrasFromDB(){}

}


public class Option : Derivative
```

```
{
  public Option(string symbol):base(symbol)
  {
  }
  public Option(Hashtable h):base(h)
  {
  }
  public string putCallType{ get {return (string)_deriv
    Attrib["putCall"];}}
  public string usEuro{ get {return (string)
    _derivAttrib ["usEuro"];}}

  protected override void loadExtrasFromDB()
  {
    string sql = "select putCall,euroUSType from
      tblProduct where pSymbol = ' " + base.symbol
      + " ' ";
    DBHandler db = new DBHandler();
    DataSet ds = db.dbSelect(sql);
    DataRow dr = ds.Tables[0].Rows[0];
    _derivAttrib.Add("putCall",(dr["putCall"].ToString
      ()).Substring(0,1).ToLower());

_derivAttrib.Add("usEuro",(dr["euroUSType"].ToString
  ()).Substring(0,1).ToLower());
  }
}

public class Future : Derivative
{
  public Future(string symbol):base(symbol)
  {
  }
  public Future(Hashtable h):base(h)
  {
  }
  public string contract{ get{return
    (string)_derivAttrib["contract"];}}

  protected override void loadExtrasFromDB()
```

```
   {
      string sql = "select contractSize from tblProduct
      where pSymbol = '" + base.symbol + "'";
      DBHandler db = new DBHandler();
      DataSet ds = db.dbSelect(sql);
      Console.Write(sql);
      DataRow dr = ds.Tables[0].Rows[0];
      _derivAttrib.Add("contract",(int)dr["contractSize"]);

   }
}
```

3.2.2 Interfaces

[access] *interface* name *{code body}*

Interfaces describe the behaviour of a class as a set of methods, properties, and events. In defining an interface all the methods and properties are guaranteed in the implementation.

interface is a keyword used to define the interface in a similar way to how a class is defined. An abstract class is similar to an interface, except it uses the abstract keyword in place of the interface keyword, and for example an abstract class may contain non-virtual methods whereas an interface may only describe the methods. For a list of the important differences, see Table 3.4. The big difference is that when it comes to implementation you may only inherit one class, whereas you can inherit multiple interfaces.

Implementing interfaces

In this section interfaces are examined from a practical viewpoint and from the perspective of using inheritance in a financial application. In the

Table 3.4   Differences between abstract classes and interfaces

Description	Abstract class	Interface
Keyword	abstract	interface
May contain non-overridable methods?	Yes	No
Inheritance	Single	Multiple
Instance variables	Yes	No
Constructors	Yes	No
Include private or protected methods	Yes	No

last section we looked at the derivative products Options and Futures. As we have seen they have many common properties and behaviour but each product has specific features. Not surprisingly pricing futures and options are different but they do share some behaviour; the options are priced using the Black Scholes model and the futures get their prices from an exchange feed.

Both options and futures need some parameters to be able to get the price from either the model or a price feed, and they both have a way of returning the price. This behaviour is defined in an interface as shown in Example 3.27 in defining Iprice. Convention in C# is that interfaces are named with a capital I before the name to denote the type to be an interface.

Example 3.27: Price interface
```
public interface Iprice
{
 void setParams(string symb);
 double getPrice();
}
```

Two classes are created that inherit from Iprice and implement the methods setParams and getPrice. The syntax for inheriting from an interface is exactly the same as that from a base class, which is a colon, followed by the interface name.

There is no limit on the number of interfaces inherited, but each property and method defined must be implemented.

When implementing the methods the method name must match but there is no override keyword as in inheriting from a base class.

Example 3.28 shows how the two classes OptionsPrice and FuturePrice implement the methods setParams and getPrice. The OptionsPrice class has two private methods to compute the price in addition to implementing the methods as required by the interface.

Example 3.28: OptionsPrice and FuturePrice classes
```
public class OptionsPrice : Iprice
{
    // declare private variables
    private const double _r = 0.04; // risk free rate
    private double _S; // Stock price
    private double _T; // Days to expiry
    private double _X; // Strike
```

```csharp
private double _v; // volatility
private double _price;
private string _callPut;
private string _symb;
//
public OptionsPrice()
{
}
public void setParams(string symbol)
{
 _symb = symbol;
 Option o = new Option(_symb);
 _T   = o.expiryDays;
 _X   = o.strike;
 _callPut = o.putCallType;
 _S   = o.ulPrice;
 _v   = o.vol;
}
public double getPrice()
{
 _price = BlackScholes(_callPut,_S,_X,_T,_r,_v);
 return _price;
}
private double BlackScholes(string CallPutFlag,
 double S, double X, double T, double r, double v)
{
  double d1 = 0.0;
  double d2 = 0.0;
  double dBlackScholes = 0.0;
  try
  {
    d1 = (Math.Log(S / X) + (r + v * v / 2.0) * T) /
    (v * Math.Sqrt(T));
    d2 = d1 - v * Math.Sqrt(T);
    if (CallPutFlag.ToLower() == "c")
    {
      dBlackScholes = S * CumulativeNormal
        Distribution(d1) - X
      * Math.Exp(-r * T) * CumulativeNormal
        Distribution(d2);
```

```
      }
      else if (CallPutFlag.ToLower() == "p")
      {
        dBlackScholes = X * Math.Exp(-r * T) *
        CumulativeNormalDistribution(-d2) - S *
        CumulativeNormalDistribution(-d1);
      }
    }
      catch (System.DivideByZeroException e)
    {
      LogError eL = new LogError(e);
    }
    return dBlackScholes;
}
private double CumulativeNormalDistribution(double X)
{
    double L = 0.0;
    double K = 0.0;
    double dCND = 0.0;
    const double a1 = 0.31938153;
    const double a2 = -0.356563782;
    const double a3 = 1.781477937;
    const double a4 = -1.821255978;
    const double a5 = 1.330274429;
    const double pi = Math.PI;
    try {
    L = Math.Abs(X);
    K = 1.0 / (1.0 + 0.2316419 * L);
    dCND = 1.0 - 1.0 / Math.Sqrt(2 * pi ) *
      Math.Exp(-L * L / 2.0) * (a1 * K + a2 * K * K
      + a3 * Math.Pow(K, 3.0)+ a4 * Math.Pow(K, 4.0)
      + a5 * Math.Pow(K, 5.0));
    }
    catch (System.DivideByZeroException e)
    {
      LogError eL = new LogError(e);
    }

    if (X < 0)
    {
```

```csharp
      return 1.0 - dCND;
    }
    else
    {
      return dCND;
    }
  }
}

public class FuturesPrice : Iprice
{
  // Declare private variables
  private string _symbol;
  private double _price;
  //
  public FuturesPrice()
  {
  }
  public void setParams(string symbol)
  {
    _symbol = symbol;
  }
  public double getPrice()
  {
    // would normally subscribe to a price feed.
    DBHandler db = new DBHandler();
    string sql = "select price from tblPrices where
    pSymbol = '" + _symbol + "'";
    DataSet ds = db.dbSelect(sql);
    DataRow dr = ds.Tables[0].Rows[0];
    _price = (double)dr["price"];
    return _price;
  }
}
```

There are now two pricing classes, one for Futures and one for Options, with the same methods and constructors with a different implementation specific to the instrument type.

By using an interface to define pricing a level of consistency has been introduced to the price classes. This has obvious advantages for the maintenance of the code, particularly where the price objects are used.

A more obvious solution is to group the price objects and use the methods setParams and getPrice as generic methods irrespective of product type. This simplifies the code further as there is no need to evaluate which product is being called for a price. This is accomplished by creating a factory class that is designed to return the price for the instrument type.

Table 3.5 shows how the factory class Pricer sits on top of the pricing classes, which in turn inherit from the pricing interface.

The Pricer class as illustrated in Example 3.29 is designed to load the relevant pricing object and, taking advantage of the uniform behaviour of the classes, implements the setParams and getPrice methods.

The Pricer constructor is given the class name of the pricing class. The next step is then to use the class name to dynamically load the class. It is important that Pricer has no knowledge of the price classes, thus making it easy to add new pricing classes without having to modify Pricer. Indeed when building the application there was a need to return the price for the underlying stock, thus a StockPrice class was written. The Pricer class needed no modifications.

Table 3.5   The relationship between the price interface, price classes and the factory class

```
Pricer
```

```
Pricer (classname, symbol)
```

```
getPrice()
setParams (symbol)
```

OptionsPrice	FuturePrice	StockPrice
getPrice()	getPrice()	getPrice()
setParams (symbol)	setParams	setParams
BlackScholes (string,	(symbol)	(symbol)
double, double, double,		
double, double)		
CumulativeNormal		
Distribution (double)		

```
Iprice
```

```
getPrice()
setParams (symbol)
```

The classes are loaded dynamically by using the Reflection names-pace, where the metadata attributes can be accessed as needed at runtime. A Type object is created using the GetType method, which searches the namespace for the item requested.

Using the Type object's method InvokeMember with the Create Instance keyword, the price object is returned.

Having loaded the requested class, the methods are then available to set the parameters, setParams, and the important getPrice method to retrieve the price.

Example 3.29: Factory class Pricer

```
public class Pricer
{
  // declare private variables
  private Iprice _price;
  //
  public Pricer(string className)
  {
    Type priceType = Type.GetType("TradingApplication.
    " + className);
    _price = (Iprice)priceType.InvokeMember(className,
    BindingFlags.CreateInstance, null, null, null);
  }
  public void setParams(string symb)
  {
    _price.setParams(symb);
  }
  public double getPrice()
  {
    return _price.getPrice();
  }
}
```

Example 3.30 shows how the Pricer object is called; the variable 'price type' is held on the product table and contains the class name needed to correctly price the product. The class name is stored to the field priceType on the creation of the product.

Example 3.30: Pricer factory class used to return the price

```
string price = "0";
string priceType = dr["priceType"].ToString();
```

```
Pricer p = new Pricer(priceType);
p.setParams(dr["pSymbol"].ToString());
price = p.getPrice().ToString();
```

The factory class is a much-simplified way of getting a price for a collection of products, the other benefit being that if a further product type were to be added to the application, only the specific class would need to be written to handle it and the `Pricer` would always know how to return the correct reference.

3.2.3 Multiple threading or asynchronous programming

Those with C++ and/or Java experience may be familiar with the concepts of multi-threading. The big advantage of multiple threading or concurrent programming is that a number of requests can be issued at once leaving the main process to continue without having to wait for each request to process sequentially.

An example taken from the futures and options application is that the FX rates are loaded from a file which, depending on the network and the size of the file, could slow the application down. The best way would therefore be to kick off a new thread to read the file and load the rates to a list box, allowing the main form to continue loading.

This section will look at the concepts of multiple threading. Given that much of the C# work typically done in finance is more likely to be in creating Windows applications, the scope for asynchronous programming outside the event driven forms will be limited. It is important to understand how it works, however, as much of the underlying code of the forms and components work using multi-threaded processes.

Threads and monitor

The two key classes in multiple threading are `Thread` and `Monitor`. Threads exist in several states and are tracked by the methods of the `Monitor` class such as `Wait` and `Pulse`.

Thread states

The lifecycle of a thread is broken down into a number of states, as shown in Table 3.6.

A thread is created with the new keyword but can only be started with the method `Start`. At this point the `Thread` then enters the `Started` or `Runnable` state. The started or runnable thread is then assigned a

Table 3.6 Thread states

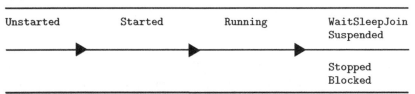

Unstarted	Started	Running	WaitSleepJoin Suspended
			Stopped Blocked

processor by the operating system. Once it starts running it executes a `ThreadStart` process; this specifies the action taken by the `Thread` during its lifecycle.

In Example 3.31 a `Thread` is initialised with a `ThreadStart` calling the `fillFXBox` method. Once initialised the `Thread` has the `IsBackground` property set to run the thread in the background; the `Thread` is set to background so that if the application crashes the CLR ensures that the `Thread` is aborted. The `Thread` is then started using the `Start` method.

Example 3.31: Process started in a new `Thread`

```
private void initializeFX()
{
 Thread fxthread = new Thread(new
  ThreadStart(fillFXBox));
 fxthread.IsBackground = true;
 fxthread.Start();
}
```

Monitor class

One of the issues in a multi-threaded program is that there may be sections of code that may only be accessed by one process at a time, for example, performing database transactions where some sort of locking will be needed to ensure data integrity. By placing `lock(object reference) {}` around a block of code enables `Monitor` to action its methods of `Enter`, `Exit`, `Pulse` and `PulseAll`.

`Monitor` locks are placed around methods as an alternative to using a 'lock block'. Once the block of code is being executed within the monitor block, then any subsequent calls must wait until the `Monitor.Exit(this)` releases the lock.

`Pulse` moves the next `Thread` back to the `Started` state; `PulseAll` moves all waiting `Threads` back to the started state.

Thread priorities

There are five values ranging from `AboveNormal` to `BelowNormal`. The `Thread` scheduler ensures the highest priority runs at all times.

3.2.4   Workshop: Exercise two

To recap on what we are trying to accomplish; the exercises take you through building an options calculator that allows a trader to enter a number of parameters and choose the valuation model. We have begun by creating a Windows application with a basic form, an option class and an option exception class. We now come to the 'guts' of the application, which calls the models to value the option. For further details on the specification and the system design please refer to Appendices A and B.

In this exercise both approaches of inheritance will be examined from a base class and from an interface. The code for the models can be seen in Appendix C where there are also details on how to download the class files.

Beginning with the design, the models take some input parameters and return a price. Write an interface `Imodel` to accept a list of parameters and return a price. This encapsulates the behaviour that was described.

Now write the base class `Model` for the models; as we have learnt base classes are very powerful when used to process common behaviour and set common properties. The two models need comparing as illustrated in Table 3.7, which will ensure that we can easily understand how they overlap and what is specific to the individual model.

The way a price is derived and returned when the models are called will vary, so we will make it a virtual class, which is overridden in the model implementation classes.

The input parameters as seen in Table 3.7 are the same and can be standardised in the form of an `ArrayList` that is fed into the individual

Table 3.7   Comparison of the model properties and behaviour

	Black Scholes	Implicit Finite-Difference
Return a price	x	x
Volatility input	x	x
Risk free rate input	x	x
Stock price input	x	x
Put or call	x	x
Time to expiry	x	x

model classes, thus the model classes can inherit the base method of `setParameters`.

The next step is to implement the `Imodel` interface with a `BlackScholesModel` and an `ImplicitFiniteDifferenceModel` class. Once this is done we need to implement the two models using the base class `Model`.

Using Table 3.3, which shows the main differences between the abstract and the interface classes, as a guide compare the two versions of the model classes, the ones written using the interface `Imodel` and the others with the base class `Model`.

Now that the classes are created, they need linking to the Windows application by adding the code to call the models from the calculate button on the form and write the results to the read-only text box created.

3.3 SUMMARY

In this section we have looked at Object Oriented programming and how it is applied in finance. The basic class structure has been looked at, along with how constructors are written and overloaded with the advantage of being able to create an object and pass different parameters to initialise it as required.

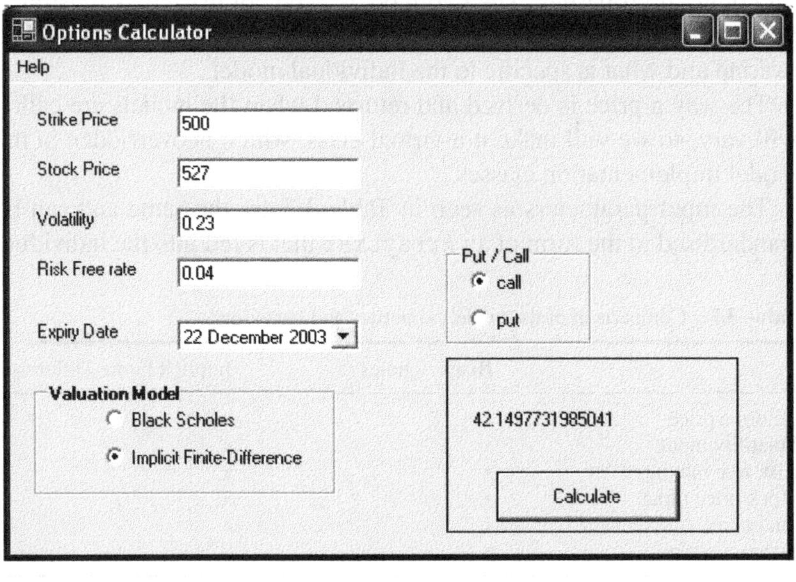

Figure 3.3 Calculator with the models implemented

Methods and properties have been explained and how the methods and properties are accessed, through the access modifiers, and it was shown how to hide variables and methods by using the private or protected keywords.

We have explored the importance of inheritance and polymorphism with a practical example of creating products. The base `Derivative` class encapsulated the common features of the futures and options allowing them to share functionality and properties. In addition to implementing the specific behaviour of the futures and options, the concept of polymorphism was introduced; this is where a `virtual` method defined in the base class is implemented for each product type using the `override` keyword.

Interfaces were then introduced as a way of guaranteeing a class structure when implemented; by defining a structure it helps greatly in readability of the code and makes maintenance of code easier.

In implementing the `Iprice` interface the two classes `OptionPrice` and `FuturesPrice` have differing levels of complexity in classes but a unified set of methods as defined by the interface. With the unified methods, this meant that a factory class could be created to manage the classes and provide a single point of access irrespective of the product type. The factory class used the `Reflection` namespace to get class information in runtime and create the necessary instances.

Finally, multi-threading or asynchronous programming was examined. Much of the Windows applications written use threading extensively as through it the forms are event driven. The application of threading in the context of doing file retrieves was looked at and how to create and kick off an object in a new thread.

The use of inheritance, with base classes and interfaces, form the core of Object Oriented programming in C#. The advantages are in reusable objects which in turn cuts down on the amount of code written and makes maintenance easier. The ease of modifying existing applications is key to finance applications, which need to keep up with the evolving nature of the industry.

4

Databases

In finance, the need to retrieve or update a database is a key part of most applications. For those familiar with ADO, the big change from ADO to ADO.NET is that ADO.NET is a *disconnected* data architecture. With a disconnected data architecture the data retrieved are cached on the local machine and the database is only accessed when you need to refresh or alter the data. In the futures and options trading system, the requirement to access the database is constant, from reading product information to booking trades and positions.

ADO.NET includes classes to handle SQL server and OLE compliant databases such as Access, but to work with ODBC compliant databases such as Sybase, you will need to download the ODBC .NET Data Provider from the Microsoft website.

4.1   ADO.NET OBJECT MODEL

`DataAdapter` and `DataSet` objects are the two key objects for managing data. The two objects split the logic of handling data into sections; `DataSet` manages the client end and `DataAdapter` manages the `DataSet` with the data source. `Data Adapter` is responsible for the synchronisation, where applicable, and has the methods to interact with the database directly.

`DataSet` is not just representation of data retrieved from a table; it also handles relationships `DataRelations`, `Constraints`, and `Tables` collections. The data cannot be directly accessed through the `DataSet`; instead a `DataTable` is returned that contains a collection of `Rows` and a collection of `Columns`.

Note: `DataSets` can also be used to create 'data source-less' tables, which can be handy for client-side temporary data or working with XML documents.

4.2   CONNECTING TO THE DATABASE

There are several `DataAdapter` classes: the `SqlDataAdapter` for use with Microsoft's SQL server; the `OleDbDataAdapter` for OLE compatible databases (both these are included with Visual Studio .NET); and the `OdbcDataAdapter` used with ODBC compliant databases.

All are instantiated in the same way as shown in Example 4.1 where a connection is made to a Microsoft SQL server and one to a Sybase database.

Example 4.1: Instantiating `DataAdapter` classes
```
SqlDataAdapter sqlDA = new SqlDataAdapter
(sqlCommand, sqlConnection);
OdbcDataAdapter sybaseDA = new
 OdbcDataAdapter(sqlCommand, sqlConnection);
```

The relevant references to the database type classes must be included at the top of the class as shown in Example 4.2.

Example 4.2: References to the various data classes
```
using System.Data.SqlClient;
using System.Data.OleDb;
using Microsoft.Data.Odbc;
```

`sqlConnection` is the string used to configure the connection to the database; this varies between providers as to the information that is required to connect to the databases.

`sqlCommand` is used to pass a string of SQL, such as a stored procedure name or `sql select` statement.

Once the `DataAdapter` has been created, the next step is to create a `DataSet` as a container for the data retrieved as shown in Example 4.3.

Example 4.3: Creating `DataSets`
```
DataSet sqlDS = new DataSet();
DataSet sybaseDS = new DataSet();
```

Once the `DataSets` have been created using the `Fill` method of the `DataAdapter`, object rows of data are added to the `DataSet` as specified in the `sqlCommand` illustrated in Example 4.4.

Example 4.4: Loading the `DataSet` with data
```
sqlDA.Fill(sqlDS);
sybaseDA.Fill(sybaseDS);
```

Table 4.2 in section 4.5 illustrates how the various classes interconnect.

4.3   CONNECTION POOLS

The overheads of connecting to a database are often higher than running a short query. With this in mind there are advantages to keeping a number of database connections alive in a connection pool and returning a connection when needed.

An abstract class creates and manages the pool and a singleton class returns a connection. Table 4.1 shows the relation between the abstract class and the singleton.

Table 4.1   Singleton connection pool class and the abstract DBConnection class

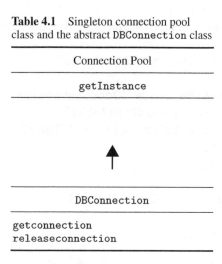

Connection Pool
getInstance

DBConnection
getconnection releaseconnection

The constructor of the abstract class DBConnection (see Example 4.5) creates a number of connections and adds them to an ArrayList of connections. There are two public methods: to get a connection and to release a connection back to the pool.[1] If the request for a connection is received and there are no more connections available then a new connection is initialised and added to the ArrayList. The ability to add connections when needed is important as the calling objects depend on getting a connection.

Example 4.5: Database connection management class
```
public abstract class DBConnection
{
    private ArrayList_connectionPool = new
    ArrayList();
```

---

[1] This is a very simple example; in practice the initial number of connections and the DSN name would not be hard-coded but derived from a file. This can be extended to handle a number of different databases and the methods to get and return a connection would need expanding.

```csharp
private int_nextAvailable = 0;
private const int_initialPool = 3;
//
public DBConnection()
{
  initConnections();
}
public OdbcConnection getConnection()
{
  _nextAvailable++;
  if (_connectionPool.Capacity <=_nextAvailable)
 {
    addConnection(_nextAvailable);
 }
  OdbcConnection con = (OdbcConnection)_
  connectionPool[_nextAvailable];
  if (con.State.ToString() == "Closed")
   con.Open();
  return con;
}
public void releaseConnection()
{
  _nextAvailable--;
}
private void initConnections()
{
    for(int i=0;i<_initialPool;i++)
    {
      addConnection(i);
    }
}
private void addConnection(int i)
{
    string dsn = "DSN=TradingApp";
    _connectionPool.Add(new OdbcConnection(dsn));
}
}
```

With the base class having been written, the next step is to wrap it around a singleton class as shown in Example 4.6 and this is how the connection pool holds the connections.

With a default or public constructor, if a new instance of the connection is created then the connections to the database are created each time thus defeating the purpose of a pool. With a singleton the constructor is made private and the only way to get a connection is through the GetInstance method, which returns a ConnectPool object that is held or creates one as required. Note the class access modifier is set to sealed to prevent this class being inherited and the constructor or methods overridden.

Example 4.6: Singleton ConnectPool class

```
sealed class ConnectPool :
  TradingApplication.DBConnection
{
  private ConnectPool()
  {
  }
  public static ConnectPool GetInstance()
  {
    if (con == null)
    {
      con = new ConnectPool();
    }
    return con;
  }
  private static ConnectPool con;
}
```

The ConnectPool is created and deployed as shown in Example 4.7. The ConnectPool object is created using the method GetInstance, the connection returned and at the end of the method the connection is released in the finally block.

Example 4.7: Connection pool being used in the dbSelect method

```
 public  DataSet  dbSelect(string sqlstr)
{
  ConnectPool c = ConnectPool.GetInstance();
  OdbcConnection con = c.getConnection();
  DataSet DSet = new DataSet();
  try
  {
    _dbAdapter.SelectCommand = con.CreateCommand();
    _dbAdapter.SelectCommand.CommandText = sqlstr;
    _dbAdapter.Fill(DSet);
```

```
}
catch (OdbcException dbE)
{
  LogError eLog = new LogError(dbE);
  eLog.writeErr(sqlstr);
  DSet = null;
}
finally
{
  c.releaseConnection();
}
return DSet;
}
```

4.4   DATABASE HANDLER

As the database components lend themselves to a good deal of flexibility, the downside is that it can be a little complicated. There are components to drag and drop onto a form to handle data as well as the classes to communicate directly with the database.

By wrapping up the functionality into a class, as shown in Example 4.8, the database calls can be simplified. There are four methods, select, insert, update and delete, with the select method returning the data as DataSet.

Example 4.8: A database handler class
```
public class DBHandler
{
  // Declare private variables
  private OdbcDataAdapter_dbAdapter = new
   OdbcDataAdapter();
  private System.Data.DataSet_dbDataSet = new
   System.Data.DataSet();
  //

  public DBHandler()
  {
  }

  public DataSet dbSelect(string sqlstr)
  {
```

```
   ConnectPool c = ConnectPool.GetInstance();
   OdbcConnection con = c.getConnection();
   DataSet DSet = new DataSet();
   try
   {
     _dbAdapter.SelectCommand = con.CreateCommand();
     _dbAdapter.SelectCommand.CommandText = sqlstr;
     _dbAdapter.Fill(DSet);
   }
   catch (OdbcException dbE)
   {
      LogError eLog = new LogError(dbE);
      eLog.writeErr(sqlstr);
      DSet = null;
   }
   finally
   {
      c.releaseConnection();
   }
   return DSet;
}
public string dbInsert(string sqlstr)
{
    ConnectPool c = ConnectPool.GetInstance();
    OdbcConnection con = c.getConnection();
    string retVal ="";
    try
    {
      _dbAdapter.InsertCommand = con.CreateCommand();
      _dbAdapter.InsertCommand.CommandText = sqlstr;
      _dbAdapter.InsertCommand.ExecuteNonQuery();
    }
    catch (OdbcException dbE)
    {
      LogError logE = new LogError(dbE);
      logE.writeErr(sqlstr);
      retVal = dbE.Message;
    }
    finally
    {
      c.releaseConnection();
```

```
    }
    return retVal;
  }
  public string dbDelete(string sqlstr)
  {
    ConnectPool c = ConnectPool.GetInstance();
    OdbcConnection con = c.getConnection();
    string retVal ="";
    try
    {
      _dbAdapter.DeleteCommand = con.CreateCommand();
      _dbAdapter.DeleteCommand.CommandText = sqlstr;
      _dbAdapter.DeleteCommand.ExecuteNonQuery();
    }
    catch (OdbcException dbE)
    {
      LogError logE = new LogError(dbE);
      retVal = dbE.Message;
    }
    finally
    {
      c.releaseConnection();
    }
      return retVal;
  }

  public string dbUpdate(string sqlstr)
  {
    ConnectPool c = ConnectPool.GetInstance();
    OdbcConnection con = c.getConnection();
    string retVal ="";
    try
    {
      _dbAdapter.UpdateCommand = con.CreateCommand();
      _dbAdapter.UpdateCommand.CommandText = sqlstr;
      _dbAdapter.UpdateCommand.ExecuteNonQuery();
    }
    catch (OdbcException dbE)
    {
      LogError logE = new LogError(dbE);
      retVal = dbE.Message;
```

```
    }
    finally
    {
       c.releaseConnection();
    }
  return retVal;
  }
}
```

4.5   WORKING WITH DATA

Those of you familiar with ADO will need to move away from the RecordSet concept of .moveFirst, .moveNext and .moveLast as this is done differently in ADO.NET.

Rather than iterate through the DataSet object directly there is a series of collections that need accessing; the hierarchy is illustrated in Table 4.2. The DataSet has a collection of Tables; these in turn contain a collection of Rows and Columns. The Rows collection can be referenced by item or by number.

Table 4.2   The hierarchical relationship between DataSet, DataAdapter and the Tables, Rows, and Columns

sqlDataAdapter
OleDataAdapter
OdbcDataAdapter
DataSet
Tables
Rows
Columns

Example 4.9 shows how a DataSet is created, the DataRow extracted and the item read and stored into a string.

Example 4.9: Extracting data from a DataSet, Table, and Row collection

```
DataSet ds = pHandler.getDataByAcctCategory
   ("trading");
```

```
DataRow dr = ds.Tables[0].Rows[this.gridPositionTrade
  .CurrentRowIndex];
string cat = dr["category"].ToString();
```

Because the architecture is disconnected `DataTables` can either be created or derive from a query. `DataColumns` represent the columns of data and form a collection contained in the `DataColumnCollection`.

`DataRelations` represents relationships between tables through `DataColumn` objects. The `DataSet` object has a `relations` property which returns a `DataRelationCollection`. The `DataRelation` supplies a rich array of functionality but it does depend on well-defined indexed relational data.

4.6   TRANSACTIONS

In this section we look at how the `DataAdapter` keeps the records synchronised with the database. There are a number of methods that you may use to update or insert a record. The `DataAdapter` has `InsertCommand`, `UpdateCommand` and `DeleteCommand` to process the updates, inserts or deletes.

C# has a number of methods to update the database. For proto-typing, dragging and dropping components onto a Windows form and linking them directly to a grid will create a quick way of viewing and updating a database. However, for scalability and use within Enterprise applications the direct method of accessing the database is preferred, as the solution will be more compact.

This section will concentrate on the direct approach of creating a command or calling a stored procedure and executing it.

Looking at an update transaction in detail, as shown in Example 4.10, the `UpdateCommand` method of the `DataAdapter` is initialised with the `CreateCommand` from the ODBC data connection. The next step is to assign the `CommandText` property the string of SQL or the name of the stored procedure and any required parameters. Finally, the `ExecuteNonQuery` method is called.

Example 4.10: An update method
```
public string dbUpdate(string sqlstr)
{
  ConnectPool c = ConnectPool.GetInstance();
  OdbcConnection con = c.getConnection();
```

```
string retVal ="";
try
{
    _dbAdapter.UpdateCommand = con.CreateCommand();
    _dbAdapter.UpdateCommand.CommandText = sqlstr;
    _dbAdapter.UpdateCommand.ExecuteNonQuery();
}
catch (OdbcException dbE)
{
    LogError logE = new LogError(dbE);
    retVal = dbE.Message;
}
finally
{
    c.releaseConnection();
}
return retVal;
}
```

As discussed earlier there are several methods to update data in C#, from using the visual drag and drop on forms to hand-coding the direct communication to the data source. There is a 'middle' way of manipulating the data in a DataSet as C# provides a way of updating the data using the DataSet class and the GetChanges method. DataSet also contains the HasErrors property to ensure data integrity.

Example 4.11 shows how to update the database by passing the DataSet to the DataAdapter.

Example 4.11: Updating the database with a DataSet
```
dataAdaptDet.Update(ds,"Positions");
```

The Update method is not the final step as the AcceptChanges or RejectChanges methods must be called. Failure to do so means the DataSet will always have the changes flagged and when the DataAdapter is called it will try and commit them. This allows for error handling, as shown in Example 4.12, by placing the methods around a try/catch block, and calling the RejectChanges if a database error is thrown.

Example 4.12: Committing changes to the database

```
try
{
  dataAdaptDet.Update(ds,"Positions");
  ds.AcceptChanges();
}
catch (OdbcException dbE)
{
  ds.RejectChanges();
  MessageBox.Show(" Update not successful " +
    dbE.Message);
}
```

4.7   WORKSHOP: EXERCISE THREE

By completing the first two exercises you have a working options calculator that allows a trader to input the required parameters to value an option and then choose the model.

By introducing databases we now have a way to read from and write to a database, thus reading products created by another process and publishing prices to the database for possible use by another application.

In this chapter we have examined in detail how connections are made and how they can be handled with a pool, and how the database interaction may be wrapped up in a class.

At this point it may be useful to refer back to Example 4.6 for the connection class, Example 4.7 for the connection pool, and Example 4.9 for the database handling class. These are available to download, details of which are shown in Appendix C.

In this exercise we will concentrate on using these classes in the context of our options calculator application. You will learn how to extract the details of an option from a pull-down list from the database, and pre-load some of the parameters such as stock price and volatility. The exercise will familiarise you with the disconnected data environment, and the interaction between DataAdapter and DataSet. See Table 4.3.

First, create the connection and database handler classes. Then create a combo box on the form that displays the option description. On selection of an option, populate the stock price, volatility, risk-free rate, and put or call type fields.

Table 4.3 Data schema for Exercise three

tblOption	
symbol	string
name	string
strike	string
volatility	double
underlyingPrice	double
riskFreeRate	double
putCall	string

To handle the data retrieval it is better to encapsulate the behaviour into a class, then assigning values to the form components should be done in the form methods.

The complete code for the models and the sample calculator can be downloaded at http://www.wileyeurope.com/go/worner. Please follow the instructions on the website on how to download the code.

4.8 SUMMARY

Databases are at the centre of every finance application, and beginning with the overview of ADO.NET and connecting to the databases we have seen how the architecture is built around a disconnected data model.

There are two sets of Data Adapter classes that are included in the Visual Studio .NET IDE, one specifically for Microsoft's SQL server, the other for compatible relational databases. However, to use other databases through an ODBC, the ODBC .NET Data Provider needs downloading and adding to the project.

Connecting to databases may take up more resources and time than running a reasonably short query to a database. By creating a pool of connections the connections are held and managed by a singleton class.

The database handler class was looked at to simplify the data access methods; by encapsulating the steps needed to retrieve and modify data in a single class the various steps required are hidden.

Working with a disconnected data model, ADO.NET is different to the ADO model of moving through datasets. The collections Rows and Columns are held in the DataSet class.

Transactions were examined along with how the `DataSet` synchronises with the database. Although there are automated ways provided in C# that are useful for prototyping, there are a series of methods to update the database directly that are more suitable for Enterprise applications. Using the `UpdateCommand`, `InsertCommand`, and `DeleteCommand` properties of the `DataAdapter` object the database transactions are managed, and are well suited for either generated SQL statements or stored procedures.

5

Input & Output

Financial applications often need to handle or generate flat files originating from vendors, exchanges or legacy systems. This section will introduce you to the simpler forms of I/O – from reading files to writing from files – and covers more complex I/O topics such as serialisation. However, the more advanced topics such as socket connections and TCP/IP will not be covered here.

In C# there is a rich set of methods for handling files and passing data around in various formats, and those familiar with C++ or Java should find it is straightforward.

When you move data around you are streaming data, and the .NET framework does lots by providing abstracted files, directories, buffered, and unbuffered streams.

5.1   STREAMS

Stream is the abstract class on which other classes are built to handle reading or writing bytes to or from some storage.

FileStream is based on the abstract Stream class and performs the read and write around a file as shown in Example 5.1.

Example 5.1: FileStream method
```
private void Filer()
{
   byte[] data = new Byte[10];
   FileStream fs = new FileStream("fx.txt",
   FileMode.OpenOrCreate);
   if (fs.Length == 0)
   {
      for(int i=0;i<10;i++)
      {
         data[i] = (byte)i;
      }
```

```
    fs.Write(data,0,10);
  }
  fs.Close();
}
```

The simple FileStream is not massively efficient as it writes one byte at a time. The BufferedStream handles byte data through an internal buffer that the operating system manages and thus is more efficient.

With the BufferedStream the input and output is a Stream and the BufferedStream is written to and read from. Once finished, the BufferedStream must be flushed and then closed. The Flush method ensures that the data are actually written out to the file.

The FileStream and BufferedStream both deal with data at a byte level which gets a little unwieldy; not surprisingly, there are StreamReader and StreamWriter classes that are designed to handle text files. They support the methods ReadLine and WriteLine which are more suited to handling text.

Example 5.2 shows how the StreamWriter class is used in a simple logging method; in this case the file is opened with the Boolean flag set to true denoting that the file is to be appended to. The error message is written and the stream closed.

Example 5.2: Log writer using the StreamWriter
```
private void logWriter(string errMsg)
{
  StreamWriter logger = new StreamWriter(_logFile,true);
  logger.WriteLine(errMsg);
  logger.Close();
}
```

5.2 SERIALISATION

With streams we have seen how to write and read binary and text to and from files. Although these have a place for simple data, where you need more flexibility in storing more complex data, C# provides the means to do this using serialisation.

Serialisation converts the objects to binary when writing out and provides the means to reconstitute them when reading in. This means that you can store your data as objects and read them back in as objects.

Looking at serialisation from a practical perspective, a series of points of a yield curve need storing as an object, but before they are stored any missing points need computing. The class, as shown in Example 5.3, is marked with the [Serializable] attribute; Serialization and Deserialization are used with the binary formatters.

Example 5.3: Yield class demonstrating serialisation

```
[Serializable]
public class Yield
{
  public Yield(decimal[] curves,string CCY)
  {
    yield = curves;
      yCurve = new decimal[yield.Length];
      file = CCY + "curve.txt";
      CookCurves();
      Serialize();
  }
  private void CookCurves()
  {
    for(int i=0;i<yield.Length;i++)
    {
      try
      {
        if (yield[i]==0)
          yCurve[i] = yield[I-1]+(yield[i-1] -
            yield[i+1])/2;
        else
          yCurve[i] = yield[i];
      }
      catch (DivideByZeroException)
      {
        yCurve[i] = 0;
      }
    }
  }
  private void Serialize()
  {
    FileStream fs = new FileStream(file,FileMode
      .Open);
    BinaryFormatter bf = new BinaryFormatter();
    bf.Serialize(fs,this);
    fs.Close();
  }
```

```
public static Yield DeSerialize()
{
  FileStream fs = new FileStream(file,FileMode
   .Open);
  BinaryFormatter bf = new BinaryFormatter();
  return (Yield) bf.Deserialize(fs);
}
public decimal[] getYield()
{
  return yCurve;
}
private decimal[] yield;
private decimal[] yCurve;
private static string file;
  }
}
```

In addition to Example 5.3, it is possible to mark some data [NonSerialized] and implement IDeserializationCallBack to perform some action on the object before it is returned to the caller.

Looking at Example 5.3 you could make yCurve NonSerialized and get the object to call CookCurve on retrieval and not before the data are stored. To do this you would do the following.

Change the class to inherit the interface IDeserialization Callback as shown in Example 5.4.

Example 5.4: Class Yield inheriting IDeserializationCallback
```
[Serializable]
public class Yield : IDeserializationCallback
```

Implement the interface as shown in Example 5.5.

Example 5.5: Implementation of OnDeserialization
```
public virtual void OnDeserialization(object sender)
{
  CookCurves();
}
```

Change the private member yCurve to NonSerialized as shown in Example 5.6.

Example 5.6: Declaring the instance variable yCurve as non-serialised
[NonSerialized] private decimal[] yCurve;

The benefit of doing this is to reduce the data stored, although there is the extra overhead of calling the CookCurve method on deserialisation. The solution implemented depends on the availability of disk-space to write larger files set against the amount of processing power needed to run the CookCurve method each time the object is retrieved.

5.3   WORKSHOP: EXERCISE FOUR

Continuing with the options calculator as done in the other workshops we now look at reading and writing to files.

This workshop will be divided into two parts: the first section creates a class that handles errors and appends the error messages to a file; the second section will deal with reading a spreadsheet and parsing the values.

Create a class called LogError and overload the constructors so that it can take an exception or a string, then add a method to write the string or exception message/stack trace to a text file.

Where the CumulativeNormalDistribution is derived from the Black Scholes model there are a number of constants used to create the distribution curve; these define the shape of the normal distribution curve. As a modification to the calculator, we will introduce a read from a spreadsheet where the traders can change the shape of the curve by altering the numbers.

Either create a new class CumulativeNormalDistribution or modify the method in the Black Scholes model class to read a CSV file and use regular expressions to put the elements into an array.

The complete code for the models and the sample calculator can be downloaded at http://www.wileyeurope.com/go/worner. Please follow the instructions on the website on how to download the code.

5.4   SUMMARY

In handling files this section has looked at the low-level writing and reading bytes to the StreamReaders and StreamWriters that make it easier to deal with text files.

With serialisation it becomes simple to pass objects around and we have looked at the point at which objects are serialised, and which sections can be marked as nonserialisable. Although there is no right answer, there is the flexibility of being able to utilise disk space or memory in the solution implemented. The topic of serialising objects was examined in the context of serialising and deserialising yield curves.

The section has covered a small but relevant part of I/O handling; there are more advanced I/O features that have not been covered as these are best looked at through MSDN, or a good C# reference book.

6

XML

XML can be thought of as a way of defining data in a document made up of a series of defined tags in a hierarchical structure. XML is widespread in financial applications as a means of passing information between different systems. C# contains a rich library of XML related classes, designed to be able to read, write and more importantly to manipulate XML documents. As the XML passed around financial applications are strictly defined, they usually have DTDs or XML schemas associated with them.

6.1 SCHEMA VALIDATION

The purpose of schema validation is to ensure that the data contained in an XML document conform to the definition set out in the schema, as opposed to validating the syntax of the document tags.

The `System.Xml.Schema` namespace contains ways of creating or reading in `XmlSchemas`; the `XmlValidatingReader` and the associated methods and properties then allow the document to be read and the nodes validated.

Example 6.1 shows the generated schema from the `XMLHandler` class that writes out a `DataSet` to XML.

Example 6.1: Document schema as generated from a `DataSet`
```
<?xml version="1.0" standalone="yes" ?>
<xs:schema id="NewDataSet" xmlns=""
 xmlns:xs="http://www.w3.org/2001/XMLSchema"
xmlns:msdata="urn:schemas-microsoft-com:xml-msdata">
<xs:element name="NewDataSet" msdata:IsDataSet="true"
 msdata:Locale="en-GB">
<xs:complexType>
<xs:choice maxOccurs="unbounded">
<xs:element name="Table">
<xs:complexType>
  <xs:sequence>
    <xs:element name="category" type="xs:string"
    minOccurs="0" />
```

```
      <xs:element name="putCall" type="xs:string"
        minOccurs="0" />
      <xs:element name="pName" type="xs:string"
        minOccurs="0" />
      <xs:element name="pSymbol" type="xs:string"
        minOccurs="0" />
      <xs:element name="Acct" type="xs:int"
        minOccurs="0" />
      <xs:element name="accountName" type="xs:string"
        minOccurs="0" />
      <xs:element name="CCY" type="xs:string"
        minOccurs="0" />
      <xs:element name="Amount" type="xs:decimal"
        minOccurs="0" />
      <xs:element name="Qty" type="xs:double"
        minOccurs="0" />
      <xs:element name="LongShort" type="xs:string"
        minOccurs="0" />
      <xs:element name="FXrate" type="xs:double"
        minOccurs="0" />
      <xs:element name="BaseCCY" type="xs:string"
        minOccurs="0" />
      <xs:element name="OpenPosition" type="xs:double"
        minOccurs="0" />
      <xs:element name="priceType" type="xs:string"
        minOccurs="0" />
    </xs:sequence>
  </xs:complexType>
</xs:element>
</xs:choice>
</xs:complexType>
</xs:element>
</xs:schema>
```

6.2   XML AND ADO.NET

C# has integrated ADO.NET tightly with XML. Within ADO.NET the
DataSet class has the ability to read from and write to XML. The first
step is to populate a DataSet as seen in Chapter 4. The two methods
WriteXmlSchema, and WriteXml write out the schema and data to XML
files respectively.

Example 6.2 is taken from the XMLHandler class in the futures and options application, where the trades are exported into an XML file for use by a Risk Management system.

Example 6.2: XML handler class that writes a DataSet to XML

```
public XMLHandler(DataSet ds)
{
        ds.WriteXml(_file);
        ds.WriteXmlSchema(_schema);
}
```

This is a useful way to ship data into an XML file directly from a database; however, the structure of the XML document depends entirely on the structure of the data source. As XML documents are designed to be passed between differing systems, it is unlikely that the tag names and the structure match the underlying DataSet.

Another approach is to create a new XML document from a DataSet as shown in Example 6.3.

Example 6.3: New XML document being created from a database

```
XmlDataDocument xmlDoc = new XmlDataDocument(ds);
```

Armed with the XmlDataDocument you can now access all the elements and get to all the properties and item data. In C# you can access all the properties of the XML document such as the root name (shown in Example 6.4).

Example 6.4: XML document root name property

```
xmlDoc.DocumentElement.Name;
```

There is also the ability to read through the nodes and manipulate the data.

One of the main benefits of working with ADO.NET and XML is the ability to create a DataSet taking advantage of the disconnected data architecture, and then use the XML write functionality.

6.3   WORKSHOP: EXERCISE FIVE

In Exercise three the option information was read from a database and the values written to the form components. In this exercise an option structure is imported from an XML file.

The XML file needs the following elements:

Table 6.1   Data schema for Exercise five

name	**string**
strike	**string**
volatility	**double**
underlyingPrice	**double**
riskFreeRate	**double**
putCall	**string**

```xml
<?xml version="1.0"?>
<structuredProduct>
<option>
    <name>Abbey Natl 500</name>
    <strike>500</strike>
    <vol>0.23</vol>
    <stock>527</stock>
    <rfr>0.04</rfr>
    <expiry>Oct</expiry>
    <putCall>C</putCall>
</option>
<option>
    <name>Ftse 100 Index Option</name>
    <strike>4125</strike>
    <vol>0.25</vol>
    <stock>4252</stock>
    <rfr>0.04</rfr>
    <expiry>Oct</expiry>
    <putCall>C</putCall>
</option>
</structuredProduct>
```

Figure 6.1   Example XML layout

Create a class to handle the XML file and read and add a component onto the form to allow the user to load the data, similar to Exercise three (the database example).

Load the XML file into a `DataSet` and use the `Tables` and `Rows` collections to hold and access the data.

It is worth noting that this exercise on using XML and ADO.NET is about learning how they fit together. If you compare the database exercise with this one, you should be able to see an abstract class or interface emerging.

The complete code for the models and the sample calculator can be downloaded at `http://www.wileyeurope.com/go/worner`. Please follow the instructions on the website on how to download the code.

6.4 SUMMARY

XML has changed the ways that differing systems can pass data between each other. The classes in C# provide a rich set of tools to read, manipulate, and write to XML documents.

The XML structure is well defined and as we have seen in this section there are classes to validate data in the XML documents using the DTDs and schemas.

In its simplest form a `DataSet` can be written out to an XML document; the generated document can also have the schema written out using the `WriteXmlSchema` method.

The link between `DataSets` and XML means that there are several ways to use the in-built functionality to extract data from a data source and convert them to XML.

`www.xml.org` is a good reference site to find out more about XML structure, DTDs and schemas.

In Exercise five you will have tried out XML and ADO.NET as a way of holding the XML data for use within the options calculator.

7

Building Windows Applications

This section looks at building Windows applications. The easiest way to do this is using the Visual Studio.NET IDE. There are alternatives to using the Visual Studio.NET IDE such as Eclipse with a C# plug-in, or even with Notepad, but it would not be too productive.

7.1   CREATING A NEW PROJECT IN VISUAL STUDIO.NET

The first step is to create a new project, through the menu option File, New, Project, as shown in Figure 7.1

Select the Visual C# projects and the Windows application. At this point it is worth giving the project a sensible name and point the location to where you would like the source code and objects stored.

The Windows application automatically creates a form entitled Form1. It may not be too obvious where to change the class name and where to change the file name.

By clicking the class view and selecting Form1, you may change the Property (Name), as shown in Figure 7.2.

In C#, unlike Java, the file name does not need to match the class name, so although you have changed the class name the file name will still be Form1.cs. To change the file name, click on the Solution explorer and select the form as show in Figure 7.3.

Now that the basic project has been created, the files are in the desired location and Form1 named to something sensible, the project is ready for development, and classes can be added.

There are a number of ways to add a class to the project; through the menu Add New Item a screen drops down that allows you to select the item you wish to add including class. In addition, by right clicking on the project name in class view, as shown in Figure 7.4, there is an option to add a class.

By clicking this, a class wizard is launched as illustrated in Figure 7.5.

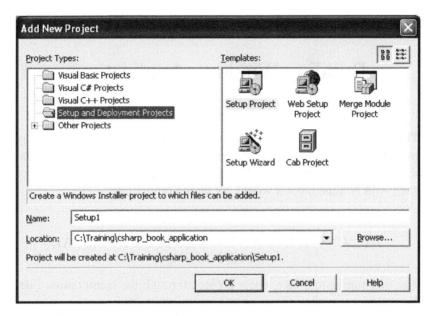

Figure 7.1   Screenshot of the new project window

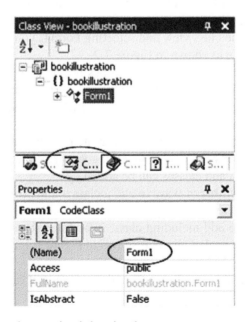

Figure 7.2   Class view panel and changing the name

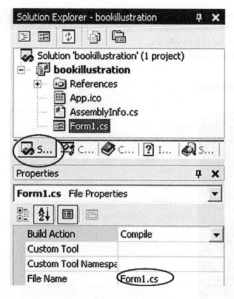

Figure 7.3   Solution explorer and changing the file name

Figure 7.4   Adding a class from the class view panel

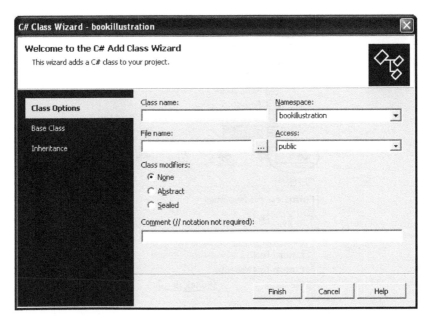

Figure 7.5   Class wizard

This wizard is handy as it allows the class name, file name, the Access modifier, and the comments to be added. In addition the Base Class option and Inheritance list the classes and interfaces available.

On clicking Finish the basic class structure is created, with the base class and/or interfaces placed in the correct place and the necessary code generated.

The generated code looks like Example 7.1.

Example 7.1: Generated code from a class creation wizard
```
namespace TradingApplication
{
   /// <summary>
   /// Base class for the hedging functionality
   /// </summary>
   public abstract class Hedger
   {
      public Hedger()
      {
         //
         // TODO: Add constructor logic here
```

```
    //
   }
  }
}
```

7.2   MANAGING PROJECTS WITH THE SOLUTION EXPLORER AND CLASS VIEW

There are two views important to managing projects in Visual Studio.NET, and to the uninitiated their precise roles may not be too obvious.

The Solution explorer is used to manage the files and references. To exclude files, rename files or indeed delete them from the project, select the file and right click; there is a menu that offers an array of options to do this, as shown in Figure 7.6. This is also the place to include references in the project because this is where the DLL files are selected and included as references.

Finally, the Solution explorer is the place to select either the code or the designer when working with forms. By right clicking on the form the options appear in a drop down menu.

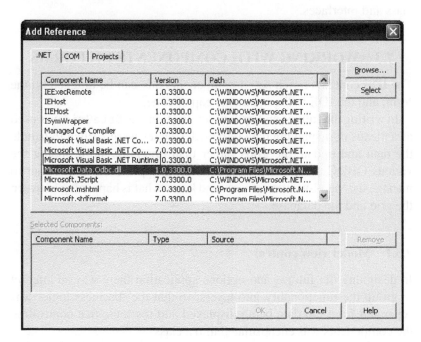

Figure 7.6   Adding a reference window

Figure 7.7   Class view showing the expanded list of methods, properties, and interfaces

The class view, shown in Figure 7.7, shows the project and the classes within the project. The view is a hierarchical representation that shows the methods and properties of the class, and where relevant the base class and interfaces.

7.3   WORKING WITH COMPONENTS ON FORMS

The IDE contains a rich set of components that can be dragged on the form, and the IDE will generate a heap of code.

In writing the futures and options application, the DataGrid was used as a means of displaying data retrieved. Classes were written to handle the data and update the grids rather than dragging and dropping the various OBDC components. For Enterprise applications it is easier to manage the 'hand-written' classes and know what is happening between the grid and the database.

7.3.1   Model view control

In designing the futures and options application there was an attempt to group the functionality into layers, so that the 'business logic' was separated from the data being displayed and the logic that controlling the components was encapsulated into a class.

Three DataGrid components were placed on the form on top of each other to represent three views of the data, the positions of the instruments, individual trades, and hedge positions.

The IDE generates the following code in the #region Windows Form Designer generated code as illustrated in Example 7.2.

Example 7.2: System generated form code

```
this.gridPositionDeriv = new System.Windows
 .Forms.DataGrid();
this.gridPositionsCust = new System.Windows
 .Forms.DataGrid();
this.gridPositionsHedge = new System.Windows
 .Forms.DataGrid();
((System.ComponentModel.ISupportInitialize)
 (this.gridPositionDeriv)).BeginInit();
((System.ComponentModel.ISupportInitialize)
 (this.gridPositionsTrades)).BeginInit();
((System.ComponentModel.ISupportInitialize)
 (this.gridPositionsHedge)).BeginInit();

//
// gridPositionDeriv
//
this.gridPositionDeriv.AlternatingBackColor =
 System.Drawing.SystemColors.ScrollBar;
this.gridPositionDeriv.BackColor = System.Drawing
 .Color.FromArgb(((System.Byte)(255)),
 ((System.Byte)(192)), ((System.Byte)(128)));
this.gridPositionDeriv.DataMember = "";
this.gridPositionDeriv.HeaderForeColor =
System.Drawing.SystemColors.ControlText;
this.gridPositionDeriv.Location = new System
 .Drawing.Point(16, 24);
this.gridPositionDeriv.Name = "gridPositionDeriv";
this.gridPositionDeriv.Size = new System.Drawing
 .Size(768, 168);
this.gridPositionDeriv.TabIndex = 0;
this.gridPositionDeriv.Click += new System
 .EventHandler(this.clickedDeriv);
//
```

```
// gridPositionsTrades
//
this.gridPositionsTrades.AlternatingBackColor =
 System.Drawing.SystemColors.ScrollBar;
this.gridPositionsTrades.BackColor = System.Drawing
 .Color.FromArgb(((System.Byte)(255)),((System.Byte)
 (192)),((System.Byte)(128)));
this.gridPositionsTrades.DataMember = "";
this.gridPositionsTrades.HeaderForeColor = System
 .Drawing.SystemColors.ControlText;
this.gridPositionsTrades.Location = new System
 .Drawing.Point(16, 24);
this.gridPositionsTrades.Name =
 "gridPositionsTrades";
this.gridPositionsTrades.Size = new System.Drawing
 .Size(760, 168);
this.gridPositionsTrades.TabIndex = 1;
this.gridPositionsTrades.Click += new System
 .EventHandler(this.clickedTrades);
//
// gridPositionsHedge
//
this.gridPositionsHedge.BackgroundColor = System
 .Drawing.Color.Gainsboro;
this.gridPositionsHedge.DataMember = "";
this.gridPositionsHedge.HeaderForeColor = System
 .Drawing.SystemColors.ControlText;
this.gridPositionsHedge.Location = new System.Drawing
 .Point(16, 24);
this.gridPositionsHedge.Name = "gridPositionsHedge";
this.gridPositionsHedge.ReadOnly =
 ((bool)(configurationAppSettings.GetValue
 ("gridPositionsHedge.ReadOnly", typeof(bool))));
this.gridPositionsHedge.Size = new System.Drawing
 .Size(768, 168);
this.gridPositionsHedge.TabIndex = 2;
this.gridPositionsHedge.Click += new System
 .EventHandler(this.clickedHedge);
((System.ComponentModel.ISupportInitialize)
 (this.gridPositionDeriv)).EndInit();
```

```
((System.ComponentModel.ISupportInitialize)
 (this.gridPositionsTrades)).EndInit();
((System.ComponentModel.ISupportInitialize)
 (this.gridPositionsHedge)).EndInit();
```

The first step was to write a method to initialise the grids and hide all but the default view, as shown in Example 7.3, and set the DataGrids to read-only as the grids are designed to only display data. The modification of the data is done elsewhere on the form and has its own set of classes that handle the transactions.

Example 7.3: Default grid display method
```
private void defaultPositionDisplay()
{
  // hide the alternate views
  gridPositionsHedge.Visible = false;
  gridPositionsTrade.Visible = false;
  gridPositionsDeriv.Visible = true;
  // Ensure Read Only
  gridPositionsHedge.ReadOnly = true;
  gridPositionsTrade.ReadOnly = true;
  gridPositionsDeriv.ReadOnly = true;
  // Now load the components
  pvcTrades.addView(gridPositionsDeriv,"grid");
  pvcCust.addView(gridPositionsTrade,"grid");
  pvcHedge.addView(gridPositionsHedge,"grid");
  // Create listeners
  pHandler.addListener(pvcTrades);
  pHandler.addListener(pvcCust);
  pHandler.addListener(pvcHedge);
  pHandler.reloadData("all");
}
```

The detail on how the model components and listeners are written is not too important at this stage. The defaultPositionDisplay method is then called in the form's constructor as shown in Example 7.4.

Example 7.4: Form constructor and the initialisation methods
```
public Form_TraderBlotter()
{
  //
```

```
// Required for Windows Form Designer support
//
InitializeComponent();
defaultPositionDisplay();
initializeFX();
}
```

Note the InitializeComponent is a generated method that is required and should not be removed.

The controller, as shown in Example 7.5, handles the updates to the grids and calls the PositionModelHandler, which returns a DataSet. The DataSet is then assigned to the DataGrid.

Example 7.5: Controller class

```
public class PositionViewController : IviewController
{
  // Declare private variables
  private Hashtable_objectCollection = new
   Hashtable();
  private string_cat;
  //
  public PositionViewController(string category)
  {
    _cat = category;
  }
  public void addView(object component,string key)
  {
    _objectCollection.Add(key,component);
  }
  public void viewUpdated(object itemUpdated)
  {
    PositionModelHandler pmh =
     (PositionModelHandler)itemUpdated;
    DataSet ds = pmh.getDataByAcctCategory(_cat);
    if (ds != null)
    {
      ((DataGrid)_objectCollection["grid"])
      .DataSource = ds.Tables[0].DefaultView;
    }
  }
}
```

The `PositionModelHandler` class, shown in Example 7.6, caches the data required for the grids and has a method to reload the data, as well as the method to return specific data from the cache.

Example 7.6: Position handler class

```
public class PositionModelHandler
{
  // private variables
  private Hashtable_dataCache = new Hashtable();
  private object[]_listeners = new object[10];
  private int_listenerCount = 0;
  //
  public PositionModelHandler()
  {
    goThroughListeners();
  }
  public DataSet getDataByAcctCategory(string cat)
  {
    return (DataSet)_dataCache[cat];
  }
  public void reloadData(string t)
  {
    if(t == "all")
    {
      initializeDS();
    }
    else
    {
      loadFromDB(t);
    }
  }
  public void addListener(IviewController o)
  {
    // change from has to some other collection
    _listeners[_listenerCount] = o;
    _listenerCount++;
  }

  private void initializeDS()
  {
    string[] categories = {"trading","cust","hedge"};
    for (int i=0;i<categories.Length;i++)
```

```
    {
      loadFromDB(categories[i]);
    }
  }
  private void loadFromDB(string category)
  {
    _dataCache.Remove(category);
    Positions pos = new Positions();
    _dataCache.Add(category,pos.
    getPositionsByCategory(category));
    goThroughListeners();
  }
  private void goThroughListeners()
  {
    for(int i=0;i<_listeners.Length-1;i++)
    {
      IviewController ivc =
      (IviewController)_listeners[i];
      if (ivc != null)
      {
        ivc.viewUpdated(this);
      }
    }
  }
}
```

A call to reloadData("all") will call the Positions class. This handles all the business logic of retrieving the data, passes a DataSet and informs the listeners that the data have been updated.

Figure 7.8 shows the data grids in action; the process of booking a ticket will trigger the reloading of the grids through the position controller.

The model view control (MVC) is a powerful mechanism to separate the business logic and the actual display logic. In this standalone application the implementation of the MVC is perhaps overcomplicated, but it is very scalable.

Let us take the trading application in a more realistic implementation, that is to say it is deployed on many desktops. There would be a mechanism that handles the trade booking and notifies the other running applications that a change has been made. Then the class that handles the messaging would update the listeners, thus notifying them that they need to do some processing.

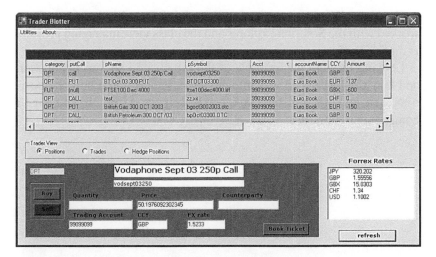

Figure 7.8   Futures and options main form showing the data grids

7.4   WORKSHOP EXERCISE SIX

Throughout this book there have been workshops proceeding towards building a simple options calculator. These exercises were designed to draw together many of the concepts examined and try and join them together.

In this exercise, to implement a Model View control would be over-engineering a simple application.

The options calculator is almost complete; the final step is to add a menu item. Write a Help menu with an About sub-menu that launches a small form with a simple 'about message'. This should familiarise you with the menu component.

The complete code for the models and the sample calculator can be downloaded at `http://www.wileyeurope.com/go/worner`. Please follow the instructions on the website on how to download the code.

7.5   SUMMARY

The Visual Studio.NET IDE is a very powerful IDE with many features. Those not familiar with the Visual Studio IDEs may find it a little tricky to get started with the IDE. A little care must be taken initially as the projects are quickly created in 'default' locations and the source files can quickly become Form1.cs, and Form2.cs which is not so meaningful.

Creating a Windows application is straightforward and once you have worked with the Solution explorer and the class view managing projects is made easy.

Looking through the example of the futures and options application and how the `DataGrid` was implemented demonstrated how the business logic and the refresh process can be separated from the `DataGrid` component on the form.

8

Deployment

Having looked at building applications, the key step of all applications is then creating a release version and deploying it.

Now for the good news – you do not need to be a maestro at registry settings or worry about conflicting DLLs.

Deployment in Visual Studio is done by adding a new project of the type 'Setup and Deployment'. You then get a number of choices of what type of setup is available, as shown in Figure 8.1.

By adding a Setup type to your project you have full control on what is shipped, registry settings, which assemblies (DLLs are shipped) and it allows you to customise the setup.

8.1 ASSEMBLIES

The base unit of .NET is an assembly; this is a collection of files that are either DLLs or EXEs. The DLLs are collections of classes and methods

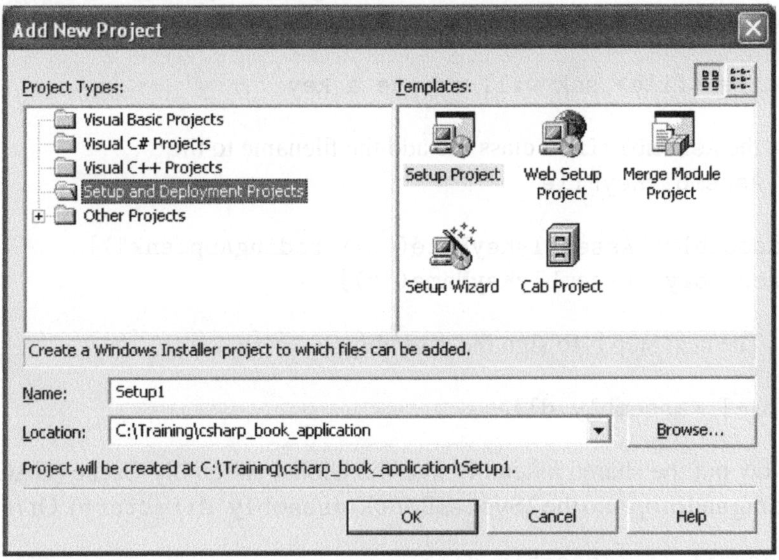

Figure 8.1 Deployment options in Visual Studio

that are used in the program and are only called when needed. Assemblies contain versioning, security and deployment information; this is held in metadata and thus negates the need for complex registry entries.

To create Multi-Module assemblies you will need to get your hands dirty with a Makefile as Visual Studio does not have the tools to do this directly from a C# project. There is a makefile wizard if you open up a blank C++ project.

8.1.1 Metadata

This is the information that is stored with an assembly that describes its methods, types and other related information. The manifest describes the assembly contents and a list of referenced assemblies. Each assembly contains version information.

8.1.2 Shared assemblies

In the olden days of PC development, applications created were very sensitive to newer versions of DLLs. Often an application that had been running perfectly happily suddenly stopped; the cause was commonly due to a newer version of a shared DLL that had been installed. In .NET this is avoided by strong names and version control.

Strong names need a unique name and have a public encryption key associated with them. To create a strong name, go to the command window in Visual Studio (view → other windows):

```
sn -k <file>.snk will create a key
```

In the AssemblyInfo class file add the filename to the AssemblyKeyFile:

```
[assembly: AssemblyKeyFile("c:\tradingApp.snk")]
[assembly: AssemblyKeyName("")]
```

The next step is to sign the assembly:

```
Sn -T <assembly.dll>
```

Now put the shared assembly into the Global Assembly Cache (GAC) (drag and drop into the %SystemRoot%\assembly directory). Or run

```
Gacutil /i <assembly.dll>
```

Now the assembly is in the shared location you can reference it in your projects.

8.2   SUMMARY

Deploying applications in the .NET framework is easier thanks to strong name and versioning and it means that intimate knowledge of registry settings is no longer required.

The ability to add a new deployment project and configure each of the install steps allows a good deal of flexibility and guarantees the applications will be installed correctly.

Bibliography

Deital, H.M., Deital, P.J., Listfield, J.A., Nieto, T.R., Yaeger, C.H. and Zlatkina, M. (2003). *C# for Experienced Programmers*. Prentice Hall, New Jersey.

Haug, E.G. (1997). *The Complete Guide To Option Pricing Formulas*. McGraw Hill, New York.

Liberty, J. (2002). *Programming C#*, 2nd Ed. O'Reilly, Sebastopol, CA, USA.

MSDN: http://msdn.microsoft.com/

Stiefel, M. and Oberg, R.J. (2002). *Application Development using C# and .Net*. Prentice Hall, New Jersey.

Wilmott, P., Howison, S., Jeff Dewynne, J. (1995). *The Mathematics of Financial Derivatives*. Cambridge University Press, Cambridge.

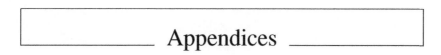

Appendices

APPENDIX A

Specification for an options calculator

The requirement is for an options calculator that takes the input required for calculating the price of an option and then on clicking the calculate button displays the price, thus allowing the options trader to quickly do 'what-if' calculations. In addition, the trader will be given the choice between the Black Scholes and the Implicit Finite-Difference models to value the options.

There is a combo box to select the option parameters from a database or the user may manually enter the parameters to retrieve a price.

The calculator has the ability to import the pricing parameters of the option to value from another system – the connection is done using XML – and again uses a combo box to select which option to load.

The cumulative normal distribution has some values imported from a comma-separated file; this allows traders the flexibility to change the distribution curve.

A diagram showing the system design is in Appendix B and the details of the model implementations in C# are shown in Appendix C.

APPENDIX B

System design

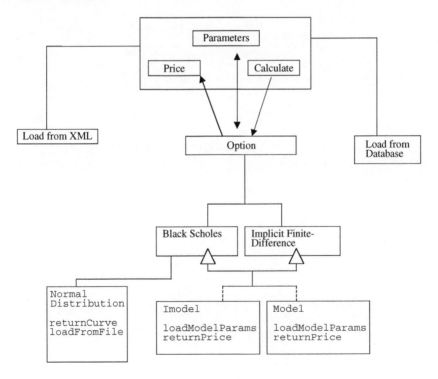

APPENDIX C

Calculation models

The two models represent different ways of valuing options. The merits of valuing options using the two models will not be discussed here as it is the subject of many financial mathematics books. The complete code for the models and workshop solution can be downloaded at http://www.wileyeurope.com/go/worner. Please follow the instructions on the website on how to download the code.

Black Scholes

Listing of the C# code.

```csharp
public class BlackScholesModel : OptionsCalculator
 .IModel
{
  // declare private variables
  private double_r; // risk free rate
  private double_S; // Stock price
  private double_T; // Days to expiry
  private double_X; // Strike
  private double_v; // volatility
  private string_callPut;

  public BlackScholesModel()
  {
  }
  public void setPricingParameters(ArrayList list)
```

```
{
  _callPut = (string)list[0];
  _S = (double)list[1];
  _X = (double)list[2];
  _T = (double)list[3]/365;
  _r = (double)list[4];
  _v = (double)list[5];
}
public double calculateOption()
{
  return BlackScholes(_callPut,_S,_X,_T,_r,_v);
}
private double BlackScholes(string CallPutFlag,
  double S, double X,
  double T, double r, double v)
{
  double d1 = 0.0;
  double d2 = 0.0;
  double dBlackScholes = 0.0;
  d1 = (Math.Log(S / X) + (r + v * v / 2.0) * T) /
  (v * Math.Sqrt(T));
  d2 = d1 - v * Math.Sqrt(T);

  if (CallPutFlag.ToLower() == "c")
  {
    CumulativeNormalDistribution CND1 = new
CumulativeNormalDistribution(d1);
    CumulativeNormalDistribution CND2 = new
CumulativeNormalDistribution(d2);
    dBlackScholes = S * CND1.curve() - X *
    Math.Exp(-r * T) *
CND2.curve();
  }
  else if (CallPutFlag.ToLower() == "p")
  {
    CumulativeNormalDistribution CND1 = new
CumulativeNormalDistribution(-d1);
    CumulativeNormalDistribution CND2 = new
CumulativeNormalDistribution(-d2);
    dBlackScholes = X * Math.Exp(-r * T) *
    CND2.curve() - S *
```

```
CND1.curve();
    }
    return dBlackScholes;
  }
}
```

Implicit Finite-Difference

Listing of the C# code.

```
public class IFDModel:IModel
{
  // Financial Parameters
  private double _S;      // Stock Price
  private double _strike; // Strike Price
  private double _T;      // Time to Expiry
  private double _v;      // Volatility
  private string _pc; // Put Call flag
  private double _rfr; // rfr
  // Mathematical Parameters
  private const double _xMin = -2;
  private const double _xMax = 1;
  private const int _xSteps = 300;
  private const int _tSteps = 50;
  private const double _tMin = 0;
  private double _tMax;
  //
  private double _dt;
  private double _dx = (_xMax-_xMin)/(double)_xSteps;
  private double _alpha;
  private double _k,_tau;
  //
  private double[] _vals = new double[_xSteps];
  private double[] _bVals = new double[_xSteps];
  private double[] _Y = new double[_xSteps];
  //
  public IFDModel()
  {
  }
  public double calculateOption()
```

```
  {
    return valueOption();
  }
  public void setPricingParameters(ArrayList list)
  {
    // Load financial variables
    _pc = (string)list[0];
    _S = (double)list[1];
    _strike = (double)list[2];
    _T = ((double)list[3])/365;
    _rfr = (double)list[4];
    _v = (double)list[5];
    // Initialize Mathematical variables
    _k = 2*_rfr/(_v*_v);
    _tMax = Math.Pow(_v,2)*_T/2;
    _dt = (_tMax-_tMin)/(double)_tSteps;
    _alpha = _dt/(_dx*_dx);
  }
  private double valueOption()
  {
// Initialize
    _tau = _tMin;
    for (int xs=0;xs<_xSteps;xs++)
    {
        _vals[xs] = payoff(xs);
    }
    // decompose the matrix
    decompose();
    // step back from expiry to current time
    for (int t=1; t<_tSteps; t++)
    {
      _tau += _dt;
      // copy vals
      for(int z=0;z<_xSteps-1;z++)
      {
        _bVals[z] = _vals[z];
      }
      // boundry conditions
      if(_pc.ToLower() == "p")
      {
        _vals[0] = _strike*(1-Math.Exp(_xMin))*
```

```
          Math.Exp(_xMin*_rfr*_tau/Math.Pow(_v,2))/
          mapper(_xMin);
        _vals[_xSteps-1] = 0;
      }
      else
      {
        _vals[_xSteps-1] = _strike*Math.Exp(_xMax)/
         mapper(_xMax);
        _vals[0]= 0;
      }
      // Adjust values next to the boundry
      _bVals[1] += _alpha*_vals[0];
      _bVals[_xSteps-2] += _alpha*_vals[_xSteps-1];
      //
      solver();
  }

      double result = 0.00;
      double x = Math.Log(_S/_strike);
      int index = (int)((x-_xMin)/_dx +0.5);
      result = mapper(x)*_vals[index];
      //
      return result;
}
private void solver()
{
  double[] holdArray = new double[_xSteps];
  holdArray[1] = _bVals[1];
  for(int i=2; i<_xSteps-1; i++)
  {
    holdArray[i] = _bVals[i] + _alpha*holdArray
    [i-1]/_Y[i-1];
  }
  _vals[_xSteps-2] = holdArray[_xSteps-2]/_Y
   [_xSteps-2];

  for (int i=_xSteps-3;i>0; --i)
  {
    _vals[i] = (holdArray[i]+_alpha*_vals
    [i+1])/_Y[i];
  }
}
```

```
private void decompose()
{
  double a2 = _alpha*_alpha;
  _Y[1] = 1+2*_alpha;
  for(int i=2; i<_xSteps-1;i++)
  {
    _Y[i] = 1+2*_alpha - a2/_Y[i-1];
  }
}

private double payoff(int i)
{
  double X = _xMin + i*_dx;
  double u = _strike*Math.Exp(X);
  double po;
  //
  if(_pc.ToLower() == "p")
  {
    po = Math.Max(_strike-u,0)/mapper(X);
  }
  else
  {
    po = Math.Max(u-_strike,0)/mapper(X);
  }
  return po;
}
private double mapper(double x)
{
  double s = _strike*Math.Exp(x);
  return_strike*Math.Exp((1-_k)*x/2 -(_k+1)*(_k+1)*
    _tau/4);
}
}
```

Index

Printed and bound by CPI Group (UK) Ltd, Croydon, CR0 4YY

23/04/2025

14660944-0005